The Poster Book of Antique Auto Ads

1898-1920

Compiled by Howard Garrett
Introduction by Lois Garrett

The Citadel Press Secaucus, N.J.

Published by Citadel Press
A division of Lyle Stuart, Inc.
120 Enterprise Ave., Secaucus, N.J. 07094
In Canada: George J. McLeod Limited
73 Bathurst St., Toronto, Ont.
Manufactured in the United States of America
ISBN 0-8065-0492-7

Introduction by Lois Garrett

1899

WHEN WE GET INTO our high-powered, smooth-riding automobiles and drive in air-conditioned comfort, we can, with the great hindsight which most of us possess, see why this wonderful invention replaced the old horse and buggy. But step back into the past and take a good look at those first motor cars. Picture yourself on a cross-country trip with Admiral Dewey in that marvelous Locomobile. Do you want to take over the steering wheel? Your first problem will be finding it. This car, like many others of that era, was controlled by a tiller which turned the car by turning the entire axle. Imagine maneuvering that! Nor was there a spare to bother with. Flat tire? Just step out, remove the tire, patch it, pump it up, put it back on, and continue over the rough, rutted, muddy or dusty road to your destination.

With all the obstacles in the way of horseless vehicles, it seems remarkable that they sold at all in the early years. But sell they did. Judging by the hundreds and hundreds of brands that were born between 1895 and 1920 it seems as though every man with mechanical ability and a bit of money and initiative was hitching his wagon (sans horse) to a star. Advertising was one way to capture the market. Many of the ads for this new-fangled, expensive item were aimed at women of all ages. Carefree young ladies, dignified suburban matrons, women with children were all shown driving these cars. This seems odd when we recall that women of that era are supposed to have been docile, domestic, subservient creatures. In spite of what we have been led to believe, advertisers obviously knew who had control of the purse strings in many a household.

Although such firms as Stanley, Pope, Winton and Duryea were producing cars in the late 1890s, it wasn't until the turn of the century that automobile ads began to appear in national magazines with any regularity. By 1905 ads were beginning to show cars with their bright paint and shiny brass trim in full color. Now, over half a century later, many of these pictures look so charming and quaint that they are worthy of being framed.

A full-column article in the May 14, 1898, issue of *Scientific American* describing the Winton Motor Carriage accompanied by a 6″x7″ picture of the car must have been a huge success. Eleven weeks later, on July 30, 1898, Winton placed its first small ad in *Scientific American*

DISPENSE WITH A HORSE

Price $1,000. *No Agents.*

and save the expense, care and anxiety of keeping it. To run a motor carriage costs about ½ cent a mile.

THE WINTON MOTOR CARRIAGE

is the best vehicle of its kind that is made. It is handsomely, strongly and yet lightly constructed and elegantly finished. Easily managed. Speed from 3 to 20 miles an hour. The hydrocarbon motor is simple and powerful. No odor, no vibration. Suspension Wire Wheels. Pneumatic Tires. Ball Bearings. ☞ *Send for Catalogue.*

THE WINTON MOTOR CARRIAGE CO., Cleveland, Ohio.

The Luxury of Locomotion

Price $1,000. *No Agents.*

is embodied in

THE WINTON MotorCarriage

They are handsome, easy riding, durable, highly economical and under perfect control.

14 of them are in actual use

and giving splendid satisfaction.

Variable Speed Hydro-Carbon Motor.

Place your order to secure prompt delivery.

☞ *Write for Catalogue.*

THE WINTON MOTOR CARRIAGE CO., Cleveland, Ohio.

Better than Horse or Bicycle

Price $1,000. *No Agents.*

One of the most delightful of modern possessions is a motor carriage. No danger of overworking a horse or of its bolting.

The Winton Motor Carriage

is in every respect a well-built conveyance. It is of pleasing design, finished in Brewster green, with leather cushions and nickel trimmings. Driving mechanism concealed. Single hydro-carbon motor. Speed from 3 to 20 miles an hour, at driver's option. Suspension Wire Wheels, Pneumatic Tires, Ball Bearings. *Price list sent free on application.*

THE WINTON MOTOR CARRIAGE CO., Cleveland, Ohio.

1898

under the heading "Dispense With a Horse." Could there be a more fitting slogan to start the first car advertising campaign? For over six years Winton placed weekly ads in the magazine, which had called the Winton Motor Carriage "so captivating as to be irresistible."

Scientific American also pointed out one of the oddities of American automobile production: Although horseless vehicles had been in common use in Europe for several years, Americans, for some reason, did not build copies of the foreign cars but perfected their own models, practically re-inventing the automobile. Much of the remainder of the text of the article appeared one sentence at a time in Winton's weekly ads. To accomplish this, slogans were changed frequently. Some ran as many as four times, others only once. Winton used these ads to boast of its great production progress. From August to November they went from fourteen to nineteen cars "in actual use." Presenting models to the public was no problem at all. In November and again in December their ads extended the invitation, "You are invited to come to Cleveland and get a ride in a Winton Motor Carriage." Anyone foolish and wealthy enough to spend $1,000 on one of those new horseless contraptions must have thought it a perfectly reasonable offer. It also makes it fairly obvious that very early automobiles were definitely considered a toy for people of means.

The unabashed snob appeal of these ads is quite startling. The Matheson was "Built for those who use the best." Lozier was "The choice of men who know." "People of good taste" chose a Chalmers, and the buyer of a 1910 Baker Electric was assured "Social prestige." Packard merely advised the buyer to "Ask the man who owns one," and posed the car against exotic backgrounds.

The Pierce Arrow, too, exuded so much confidence that by 1910 they were saying practically nothing about the car and merely showing it at various locations, including the theater, an aviation meet, and in the Great West. In many of these ads the prospective Pierce Arrow purchaser was so knowledgeable that he needed neither text nor picture of the car. The Peerless, too, advertised in this manner. Chauffeurs, mansions and elegantly dressed people were as important in getting the message across as the cars. In the early days of auto production, when it was not uncommon to purchase the chassis and body separately, De Lage, with six words and a striking illustration appealed only to those who were interested in, "De Lage La Voiture Chic, Le Chassis $12,000." One can only wonder what le rest of le car would have cost.

Any collection of early car ads also presents a history, sketchy though it may be, of the automobile itself. Thus we see that in the beginning the internal combustion engine with its sputtering and exploding wasn't the only form of

The Winton Motor Carriage

is an accomplished fact.

They are in Actual Use in half a dozen States and their owners are full of enthusiasm.

THEY ARE AVAILABLE on all roads and hills open to common traffic, at from 3 to 20 miles per hour and at a cost of ½ cent per mile.

Variable Speed Hydro-Carbon Motor, simple in construction and free from odor. ☞ *Send for Catalogue.*

Price $1,000. *No Agents.*

THE WINTON MOTOR CARRIAGE CO., Cleveland, Ohio.

The Other Fellow

can easily and successfully operate and care for a

WINTON MOTOR CARRIAGE.

Nineteen of them are daily proving this, and why not you?

They run equally well in Winter.

Hydro-carbon system, ½ cent per mile.

Price $1,000. *No Agents.*

THE WINTON MOTOR CARRIAGE CO., Cleveland, Ohio.

You Are Invited

to come to Cleveland and get a ride in a

Winton Motor Carriage

and satisfy yourself that they are a practical machine for all purposes. Winter or Summer, they are always ready for service. Hydro-carbon system, ½c. per mile.

Price $1,000. *No Agents.*

THE WINTON MOTOR CARRIAGE CO., Cleveland, Ohio.

power available to the prospective car buyer. The White steam car claimed to be "noiseless, odorless, free from vibration." The problems of tending gauges and boiler explosions were never so much as hinted at. Electric cars, too, promoted the quiet ride. Round trips as long as seventy-five or perhaps one hundred miles could be made on a single charge. In cars where neither speedometers nor odometers were standard equipment, think of the problems this could create. Small wonder that these cars were presented chiefly as town cars for ladies. And why not? What could be easier than driving a car? Baker, in 1909, was claiming, "You can learn to run the Baker in Twenty Minutes." The ladies who believed this probably gave rise to the never-ending series of jokes about women drivers. One look at the passengers in these zany electrics furthers the image of the inattentive woman driver. In cars where front and rear end are practically indistinguishable and passengers faced either direction the modern observer is unable to tell which is the driver's seat. Fortunately, in 1912, Waverley was kind enough to include a floor plan in their ads. Now, by matching the diagram carefully with the car occupants, we can see that the lady in red, head turned to the rear, is driving this car with the "full view ahead." It is possible that the shape of the car is as confusing to her as it is to us and not until she starts will she be able to discern front from rear.

Advertising techniques have changed little since the early 1900s. Anyone who has bought the top model of a car or appliance only to see it replaced two months later with an improved model can sympathize with the purchaser of a 1909 Baker Electric. This bit of "mechanical perfection," as shown in the "Queen Victoria" model, was obviously chain-driven. But, in December, when the new models were advertised, owners of the mechanically perfect chain drive learned that the new shaft drive was "noiseless at any speed," and that it "eliminates chains and chain troubles." Caveat emptor.

While some claims were silly or far-fetched, one in the *Saturday Evening Post* on October 3, 1908, probably didn't go far enough. This ad, in the same year that Pierce Arrow two- and three-passenger runabouts were selling for up to $3750, said that new production techniques, by enabling the manufacturer to produce cars in large quantity, could bring them to the public for only $850.00 f.o.b. Detroit. Thus was Henry Ford's Model T announced to the public. It remained in production for almost nineteen full years. The mass production and assembly methods created to produce this car revolutionized all forms of manufacturing throughout the world. And, by placing a true automobile, not just a mere horseless carriage, well within the reach of thousands upon thousands of Americans, Ford, more than any other man, changed the United States

1903

into the auto-oriented society it is today.

Just four years after Ford announced his Model T, cars had attained such perfection that R. E. Olds, Designer, was able to announce, "My Farewell Car." Cars, according to the man for whom both the Oldsmobile and the Reo were named, could not possibly be improved. He must have been right, since he had already created "twenty-four models in twenty-five years." This would mean he began creating self-propelled vehicles in 1888, well ahead of the first true commercial production of automobiles in the United States. One look at the "extras" listed in his ad shows how advanced the car really was. For $100 additional the purchaser received such frills as "mohair top, side curtains and slip-cover, windshield, gas tank and speedometer. Self-starter, if wanted, $25.00 extra."

Fortunately, no one, not even Olds himself, seems to have taken this ad too seriously. More and better automobiles were produced at an ever-increasing pace. Speedometers, windshields, self-starters, rear view mirrors, once luxurious extras, became integral parts of the car. The beautiful Pierce Arrow, those magnificent Marmons, the quaint electrics and hundreds of other brands now remain only as pictures or as cherished antiques. Still others, foreign and American, among them Buick, Oldsmobile, Ford, Mercedes, Fiat, Rolls-Royce, have lasted since the infancy of auto production and are still going strong.

Here, then, is an album of this baby as it was growing up, from the turn of the century until 1920. Photos, sketches, portraits by leading artists such as Frank X. Leyendecker, Louis Fancher and others are included. Marmon, Pierce Arrow, and Baker Electric are especially well represented in the color pages because of the lengthy and excellent color advertising campaigns they conducted. What appear as pretty pictures at first glance become more fascinating each time we look at them. Close observation gives us a picture of the changes in cars, in the people who drove them and in the techniques used to sell them over the years. Here is the auto at work, at play, or at rest, always lovingly and appealingly presented. From the hundreds of available ads some, like the Model T, were chosen for their historical importance, others as representatives of famous brands, but most, as in any picture album, were picked for their irresistible good looks.

The Star of the Automobile World

THE MILWAUKEE

BEAUTY DURABILITY

SERVICE STRENGTH

"THE MILWAUKEE" is built to anticipate the demands of those who are satisfied with nothing less than the best in every detail of construction, design, and adaptability to their requirements. It is handsome, strong, speedy, dependable. Our final output is the result of many months of costly experimenting. We have eliminated all fads and unnecessary appliances, even discarding some automatic devices which experience has proved to be uncertain and dangerous, and are placing vehicles on the market that can be safely and easily handled by persons of ordinary intelligence, expert engineering or mechanical knowledge not being necessary to successfully operate them. Every vehicle that leaves our factory is tested on a hill directly in front of our factory, with a rise of 80 feet in a distance of 400 feet. You need not be afraid of hills with "THE MILWAUKEE."

Write to us for descriptions and prices of any of our 20 styles of "up-to-date" pleasure vehicles and practical commercial wagons. We can prove their superiority over all others, but we must hear from you first.

The Milwaukee Automobile Co., Milwaukee, Wis.

Shippey Bros., Limtd., 13-14 King Street, London

The Stars of the Show

Again the *Ford Cars* held the "center of the stage" at the New York show. Experienced motorists were enthusiastic in praise of Henry Ford's advanced ideas, and the universal query "what has Ford this year?" emphasized the fact that the Automobile world looks to Henry Ford for the ultimate perfection of motor driven vehicles.

For 1905 we have the FORD MODEL "B" with a four-cylinder (vertical) engine, extra long wheel base, side entrance tonneau, direct drive, and an absolutely new and original idea in driving construction. Weight is 1700 lbs., and as the engine develops more than 20 H. P., it gives the car more power for its weight than any Automobile of similar type.

The Ford driving frame is such an evident advance in construction that everyone interested ought to have our new catalogue describing this wonderful Ford invention. Price of Model "B" $2000.

FORD MODEL B, PRICE $2000

FORD MODEL C, PRICE $950

The FORD MODEL "C" has a 10 H. P., double opposed motor with the successful Ford planetary transmission, a lengthened wheel base and perfect distribution of weight, making it the most practical car on the market for business or professional men or for ordinary family use. The price of Model "C" is $950, with detachable tonneau, so the car can be used as a runabout if desired.

Economy of maintenance, always a feature of the Ford cars, is further guaranteed in the 1905 Models, by light, strong construction and mechanical simplicity and excellence.

Catalogue sent on request.

Ford Motor Co., Detroit, Mich.

Canadian Trade supplied by Ford Motor Co. of Canada, Ltd., Walkerville, Ont.

1905

VISIT the palaces of America, the great country places famed for their beauty, their taste—the richness of every portion of the establishment—and you will find a C. G. V., a 50 H. P. or 75 H. P. touring car. It is the last touch, the finishing detail that marks the class of its owner as definitely and as unmistakably as an hundred Bradstreets or Almanacs de Gotha.

WHEN the list of men who drive one make of car includes a long list of the world's greatest financiers, then the supremacy of that car is definitely established. Those men have every opportunity of finding out just which car is the best in every way—and they do find out before they buy. Their brains and their resources forbid the unforgiveable mistake of accepting any but the best.

A SPEED of 80 miles an hour; unlimited power, the most that the world has ever yet produced in motor car beauty, comfort, convenience, splendor and luxury; these are a few of the points of the C. G. V. These are a few of the reasons why the C. G. V. is brought from France to this country, to England, to Germany, to St. Petersburg, to Rome, to Castile, to Carracas, to Vienna, to Sydney, to wherever a man has decided he will have that one car, which, beyond all doubt, is the greatest car in the world.

Many other points are embraced in our Catalog No. 28. Send for it; it's free.

Among the many prominent Americans now driving the C. G. V. are
W. Waldorf Astor, Mrs. Ogden Goelet, James Gordon Bennett,
O. H. P. Belmont, Whitelaw Reid, The Duchess of Roxburgh,
Clarence Mackay, W. K. Vanderbilt, Countess Boni de Castellane,
Oliver Iselin, Jr., Chas. M. Schwab, Frank J. Gould.

SOLE IMPORTERS FOR UNITED STATES AND CANADA

C. G. V. IMPORT COMPANY

1849 Broadway, at 61st Street, New York City

1907

The new, four-cylinder
26 H. P.
"Maxwell"
at $1750
marks a new epoch in automobile history

THIS splendid car—an exact duplicate, as to mechanical principles, of the famous 4-cylinder "Maxwell" which won the Deming Trophy in the Glidden Tour of 1906, and served as pilot car in the 1907 Glidden Tour—supplies, for the first time since automobiles were invented, all the efficiency of the extravagantly-priced cars at low cost.

Just think of this high-powered car, comprising all the well known and time-tried principles of the "Maxwell," selling at only $1750!

THIS NEW "MAXWELL" WONDER

is a worthy addition to the "Maxwell" line. It embodies the famous "Maxwell" principles of thermo-syphon cooling, without pump; all metal multiple-disc clutch; three-point suspension, and eliminates excessive weight, thus so notably keeping down the cost of maintenance.

The great point for the prospective buyer to remember is that this 26 H. P. "Maxwell" performs every possible service required of the largest cars. The "Maxwell" record has been one long series of triumphs in endurance contests, hill-climbing contests, &c. If you don't know the "Maxwell," you don't know the best automobile value in the world. Over seven thousand five hundred delighted "Maxwell" owners testify to "Maxwell" supremacy. The 12-14 H. P. Tourabout costs only $825, and the 16-20 H. P. Touring Car, fully equipped, only $1450.

Benj Briscoe

President, Maxwell-Briscoe Motor Co.

Address Department 37

for a complete "Maxwell" catalogue, and kindly address me personally for a personal letter of introduction to the "Maxwell" dealer nearest you, for a "Maxwell" ride over the most stubborn hill or toughest piece of road that you know.

Members A. M. C. M. A. **15 Park St., Tarrytown, N. Y.**

Main Plant: **Tarrytown, N. Y.** *Dealers in all large cities* *Factories:* **Chicago, Ill. / Pawtucket, R. I.**

THE "MAXWELL" IS EXHIBITED ONLY AT GRAND CENTRAL PALACE, NEW YORK, OCTOBER 24-31

1907

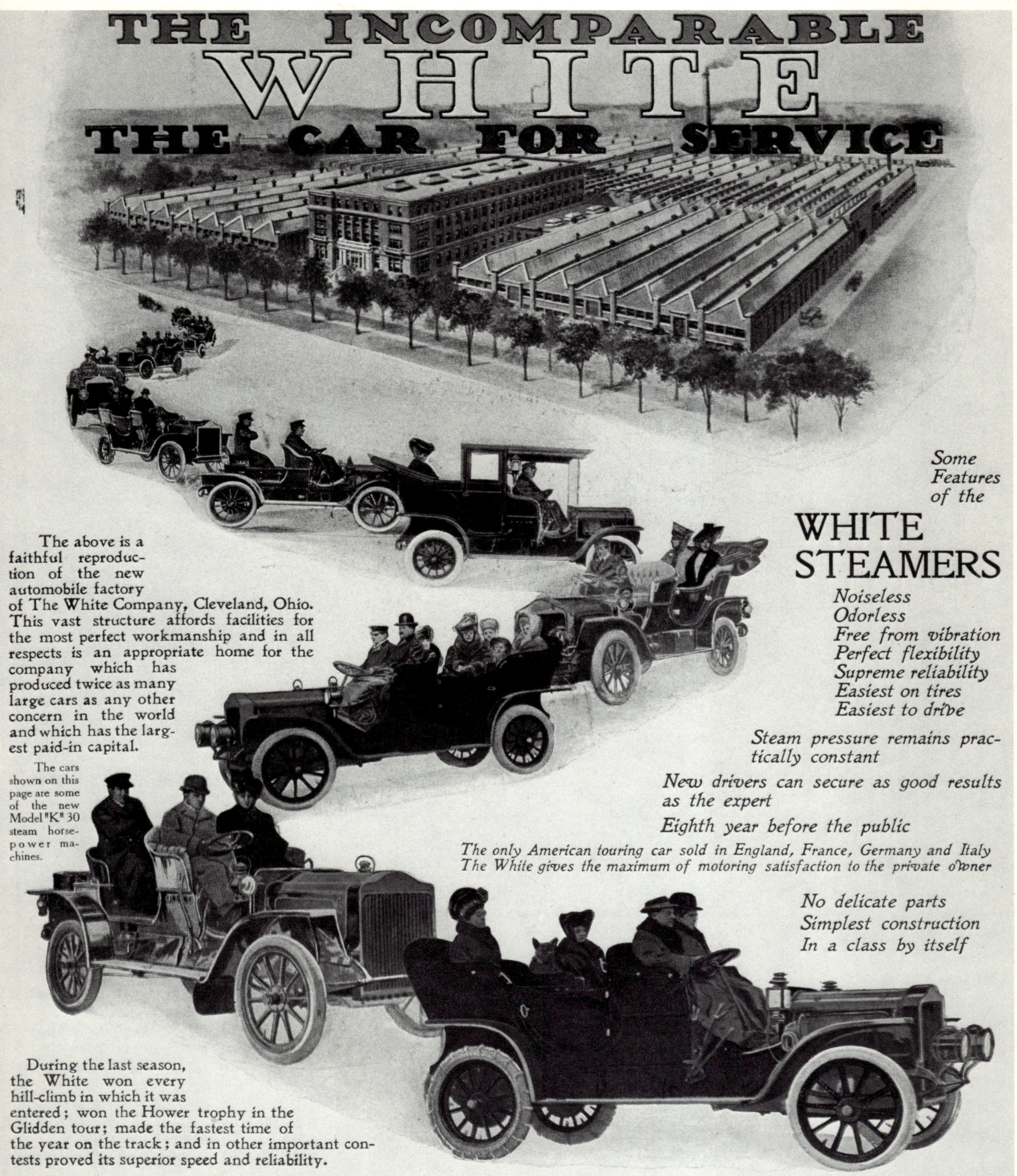
THE INCOMPARABLE
WHITE
THE CAR FOR SERVICE
The above is a faithful reproduction of the new automobile factory of The White Company, Cleveland, Ohio. This vast structure affords facilities for the most perfect workmanship and in all respects is an appropriate home for the company which has produced twice as many large cars as any other concern in the world and which has the largest paid-in capital.
The cars shown on this page are some of the new Model "K" 30 steam horse-power machines.
Some Features of the
WHITE STEAMERS
Noiseless
Odorless
Free from vibration
Perfect flexibility
Supreme reliability
Easiest on tires
Easiest to drive
Steam pressure remains practically constant
New drivers can secure as good results as the expert
Eighth year before the public
The only American touring car sold in England, France, Germany and Italy
The White gives the maximum of motoring satisfaction to the private owner
No delicate parts
Simplest construction
In a class by itself
During the last season, the White won every hill-climb in which it was entered; won the Hower trophy in the Glidden tour; made the fastest time of the year on the track; and in other important contests proved its superior speed and reliability.
THE WHITE COMPANY
CLEVELAND, OHIO

1907

Ford HIGH PRICED QUALITY
IN A LOW PRICED CAR
The Ford Four Cylinder, Twenty Horse Power, Five Passenger Touring Car $850.00 Fob. Detroit
THE one real automobile value among all the "season sensation" announcements is this big, roomy, powerful five-passenger touring car at the hitherto unheard of price of $850.00. A car that possesses at least equal value with any "1909" car announced, and at the same time sells for several hundred dollars less than the lowest of the rest.
Compare the following features of the new Ford car with those of any higher priced car offered and see if you can justify in your own mind the additional expenditure that buying any other car involves.
The Model T is a 4-cylinder, 20 h. p., five-passenger family car—powerful, speedy and enduring,—a car that looks good and is as good as it looks. Built in our own shops, it is not an "assembled" car.
It is supplied with a unit power plant—and the magneto is an integral part of same, a guaranteed troubleless magneto,—cylinders are cast in one block with detachable head, rendering all parts easily accessible.
A 3-bearing crank shaft insures perfect alignment. A cam shaft with 8 cams integral, guarantees proper valve operation. Crank and cam shafts drop-forged, each from a single non-welded Vanadium steel ingot.
Steering gear on left-hand side,—the logical side for American roads.
Car is shaft driven through one universal joint to Ford system of final drive. Patented in all countries. The system acknowledged to be the only adequate solution of the problem of delivering power to the wheels.
Vanadium steel is used throughout the entire car wherever strength is necessary. The axles, shafts, connecting rods, springs, gears, brackets, etc., are all of Vanadium steel,—each from a separate formula and all especially heat-treated in our own plant and from our own analyses. We defy anyone to break a Ford Vanadium steel part with any test or strain less than 50% greater than is required to put any other special automobile steel entirely out of business.
The weight of the car is only 1,200 lbs.—brought about by scientific construction and the use of Vanadium steel. Not an ounce of necessary weight sacrificed, not an ounce of dead weight in the car.
The importance of this light weight is vast. M. Michelin, noted tire expert, in a paper recently read before the French Society of Civil Engineers, said: "The total travel of which a tire is capable is inversely proportional to the cube of the weight which it carries." If the load is doubled the average wear and tear is multiplied by eight, if the weight of the car is increased 33⅓% the life of the tire is decreased one-half. The effect on gasoline and oil consumption and the need for repairs is similar.
That is one of the reasons the Ford car will run more miles for less money than any other touring car manufactured.
One-hundred-inch wheel base, 56-inch tread, 30-inch wheels, 3½-inch tire rear, 3-inch front; gasoline capacity, 10 gallons—225 to 250 miles; long, clean-cut lines throughout, handsomely finished, and you have the specifications on the real automobile value of this year and next and a couple more thereafter.
We make no apologies for the price,—any car now selling up to several hundred dollars more could, if built from Ford design, in the Ford factory, by Ford methods, and in Ford quantities, be sold for the Ford price if the makers were satisfied with the Ford profit per car.
Your guarantee that this car is all we claim—and our claims are broad—is in the reputation of Henry Ford, who never designed or built a failure, and in the reputation of the Ford Motor Company, who have built $20,000,000.00 worth of successful cars of Ford design in the same factory, with the same organization and system, and bearing the same imprint that the Model T is manufactured under. It's the guarantee of works as well as words.
Delivery began October 1st, orders filled in rotation. Cars can be seen at all branch stores; get a demonstration if you are near by, if not, wire your order either for immediate shipment or definite future delivery.
FURTHER details in catalog, which is yours for the asking.
Ford Motor Company
266 Piquette Ave.
Detroit
BRANCHES:—
New York, Boston, Philadelphia, Buffalo, Cleveland, Chicago, St. Louis, Kansas City, Denver, Seattle.
Paris, France. London, England. Canadian Trade:—Ford Motor Company, of Canada, Ltd. Walkerville Ont. Branch, Toronto.
Ford

1908

45 H. P. 4-Cylinder Touring Car

Every HOTCHKISS is a mechanical MASTERPIECE. Yet the Hotchkiss competes in price with the cars of America. Think of it! The greatest automobile of France at the price of a *merely good* American machine.

Every HOTCHKISS Car embodies the same exquisite refinement in metals, the same accurate attention to minute detail, the same mathematical precision in workmanship that have won fame for the HOTCHKISS RAPID FIRE GUNS in the armies and navies of the world. Every HOTCHKISS CAR is a worthy product of the most skillful and experienced engineers and craftsmen and the finest equipped factory in France.

CHASSIS PRICES ON '08 MODELS ARE:

65 H. P. 6 Cylinders, two to seventy miles an hour on high gear,	**$6,500.00**
45 H. P. 4 Cylinders, four to sixty miles an hour on high gear,	**5,000.00**
Town Car, 16-20 H. P. - - - - - - - - -	**3,500.00**

21,250 Miles in 168 Consecutive Days over Unpicked Roads

A regular stock 6-cylinder HOTCHKISS in an officially supervised tour over unpicked roads of England, Ireland, Scotland, Wales, and France covered 21,250 miles in 168 consecutive days, establishing the World's Record for Reliability. Average per day for repairs, six minutes. At end of tour £9 sterling ($45.00) on repairs put the car in perfect condition. Send for brochure, "The Hotchkiss Tour," giving minute details of this historical endurance test.

HOTCHKISS IMPORT COMPANY

Sole Concessionnaire for United States 1855 Broadway, at 61st Street, NEW YORK CITY

We require representation for the HOTCHKISS in a number of important cities. Write for particulars.

THE 1909

Packard "THIRTY"

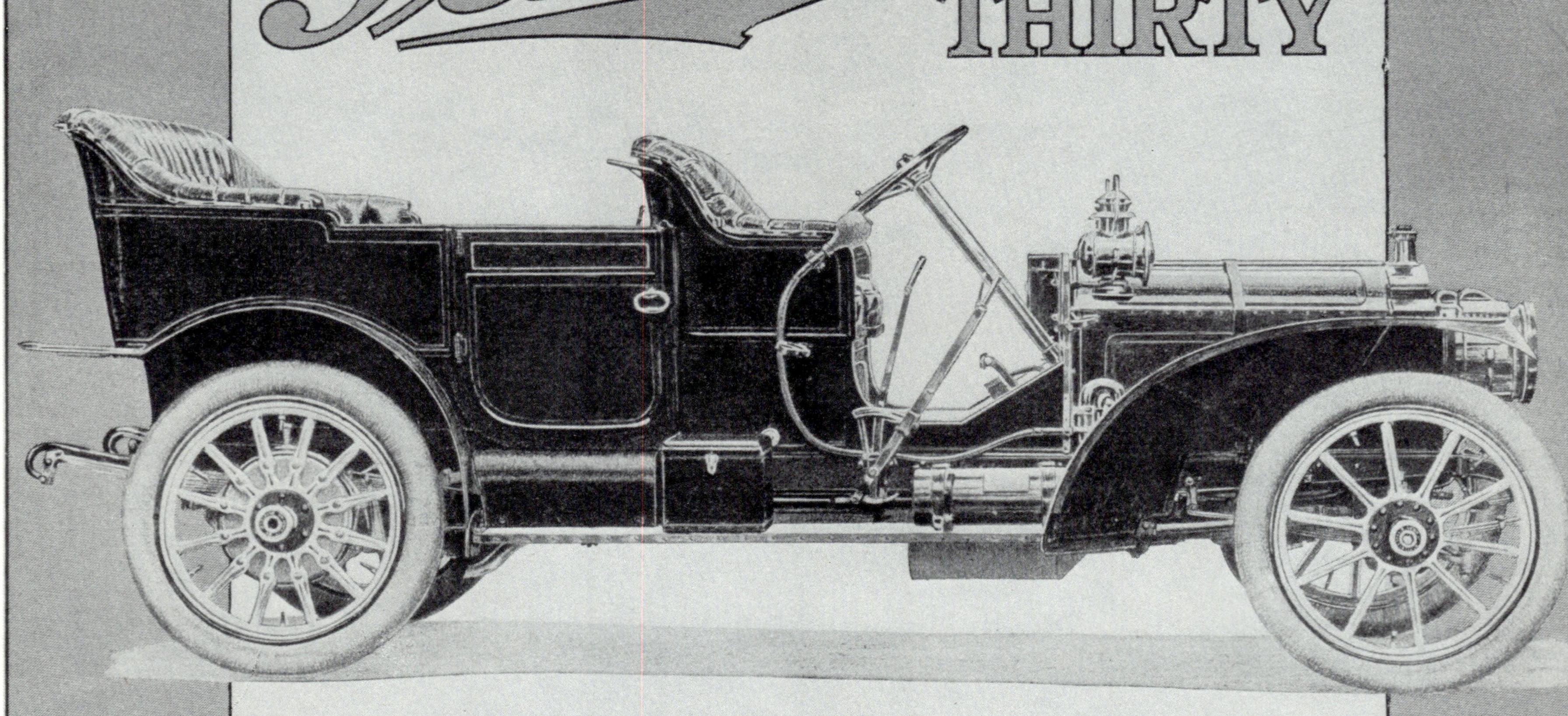

Touring Car, in Standard Finish
and Equipment, $4,200

Touring Car — Runabout
Limousine — Landaulet
Other Bodies — Chassis

Manufactured Entirely
in the Packard Shops

"Ask the man who owns one"

Packard Motor Car Company
Detroit, Michigan

1908

WHEN EQUIPPED with regular rear seat, a light four-passenger touring car; rear seat removed (can be done in a moment) and rumble seat substituted, a smart runabout; without rear or rumble seat, a combination passenger and baggage car.

A necessary adjunct to every suburban or country home

The Studebaker "Suburban" is adaptable to numerous uses that will readily suggest themselves.

For instance: When your home is located at a distance from the railway station and you have a visitor arriving on a late train, you can remove the rear seat and, if you wish, bring home your visitor and his baggage in one trip; or, if there is a party you can send your man back to the station for their baggage.

Your baggage can be carried to the beach in your "Suburban."

It is just the car for a hunting, fishing or other outing trip, for running out to the golf or country club as a light four-passenger touring car or as a smart runabout.

The Studebaker "Suburban" is a car you will use every day in half a dozen different ways — it is literally the *adaptable* car.

The Studebaker "Suburban" chassis is identical with that of the regular Studebaker "30" touring car, which is a sufficient guarantee that from a mechanical standpoint the car will give satisfactory service.

Write for full description of the Studebaker "Suburban" and other gasolene and electric models.

Studebaker Automobile Co., Main Factory South Bend, Ind. General Office Cleveland, O.

BRANCHES:

Boston, Mass.—Studebaker Bros. Co. of New York, 1020 Boylston Street (Sub Branch)
Chicago, Ill.—Studebaker Bros. Mfg. Co., 378-388 Wabash Avenue
Cleveland, Ohio—Studebaker Automobile Co., 2064 Euclid Avenue
Dallas, Texas—Studebaker Bros. Mfg. Co., 317-319 Elm Street
Denver, Colo.—Studebaker Automobile Co., 1536 Broadway
Kansas City, Mo—Studebaker Bros. Mfg. Co., 13th and Hickory Streets
New York City—Studebaker Bros. Co. of New York, Broadway and 48th Street
Philadelphia, Pa.—Studebaker Bros. Co. of New York, 330 North Broad Street (Sub Branch)
Portland, Ore.—Studebaker Bros. Co. Northwest, 330-336 East Morrison Street
Salt Lake City, Utah—Studebaker Bros. Co. of Utah, 157 State Street
San Francisco, Cal.—Studebaker Bros. Co. of California, Mission and Fremont Streets
Seattle, Wash.—Studebaker Bros. Co. Northwest, 308 First Avenue, So. (Sub Branch)

1908

This is the car that has rendered other electric types obsolete:
THE Detroit ELECTRIC
Let us recapitulate briefly some of the points which have won first place for the Detroit Electric, almost by common consent.
Here in Detroit — the automobile center of America — the Detroit has displaced all other models.
Here, and in every community of consequence, it is the chosen car of the electrical engineer, the builder of gas cars — the men of technical and practical experience.
How has this come to pass?
The picture practically answers this question.
It shows a car of surpassing elegance and dignity.
It shows that the Detroit door opens to the front instead of the rear —
The step pads are oval instead of having sharp square corners —
The cushions are more luxurious; the rear one 20 inches deep; the front one 15 inches. The deepest you have ever seen in an electric are 18 and 19, 13 and 14 inches —
The curved front windows are larger; there is nothing whatever to obscure the operator's vision at any angle —
The grab handles on the doors — and all trimmings — are silver finished.
So much — although these are only the more important points — that makes for perfect ease and luxury in the Detroit.
Let us look over the mechanical and operating details.
The battery is larger and more powerful.
You get more mileage and greater speed — many a Detroit owner, in continuous every-day service, is getting a consistent average of 85 miles; and 100 miles is easily possible.
You have five speeds forward and one reverse. You had thought three forward and one reverse the ultimate limit.
Speed control, the alarm and motor brake are concentrated in one lever — simplest and easiest control.
Mounting the motor under the body in the center of the frame removes undue weight and strain from the rear axle and tires.
We could go on enumerating full fifty distinctive Detroit features, improvements which make for efficiency and economy of operation.
As it is, haven't we told you enough to show you conclusively what a splendid carriage the Detroit is — how much better than the finest and best you have seen in other makes?
Write for the literature — especially the book which describes and pictures this car's unprecedented 1060-mile road tour from Detroit to Atlantic City.
Anderson Carriage Company
Dept. B, Detroit, Mich.

1909

THE GREAT
ARROW

TRE

1907

1908

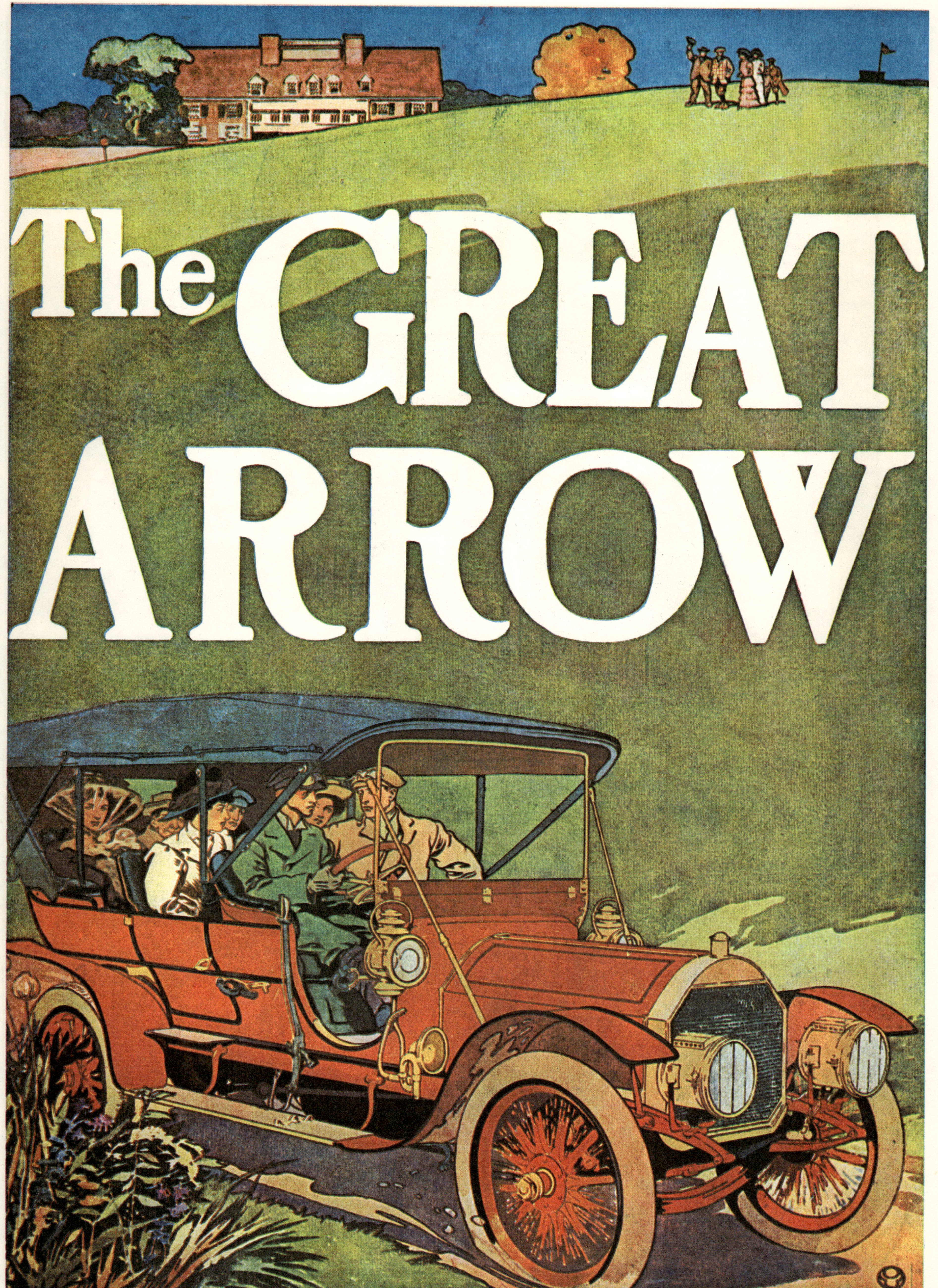

1907

Baker Electric Vehicles

The Aristocrats of Motordom

The Electric that Meets Every Need of the

SOCIETY WOMAN

You can learn to run The Baker in 20 minutes. It far exceeds all other electrics in simplicity, safety, as well as mileage and speed. It is noiseless and clean; having a battery capacity of 70 to 100 miles, it is unequalled for city and suburban use.

Write for Our Handsome Booklet

It clearly explains the many advantages of Baker Electrics, and gives full information regarding the elegant 1910 MODEL Coupes, Broughams, Victorias, Landaulets, Roadsters, etc.

THE BAKER MOTOR VEHICLE CO., 39 WEST 80TH STREET, CLEVELAND, OHIO

Salesrooms in the Principal Cities

1909

Model 32 Six-Cylinder Fifty Horse-power Torpedo

Under stress of hard service the Peerless maintains a smooth and uninterrupted action, and when judged by the highest esthetic standards it elicits nothing but intelligent admiration

The Peerless Motor Car Company, 2443 East 93d Street, Cleveland, Ohio

Licensed under Selden Patent

1910

The Triumph of the Locomobile

The finish of the 1908 International Race for the Vanderbilt Cup. Won by the 90 H.P. Locomobile at an average speed of 64.38 miles an hour, breaking all records established in competition for this celebrated trophy. A victory for the Locomobile—a triumph for the entire American automobile industry. The striking poster illustrated above is lithographed in eleven colors. Suitable for framing, with or without descriptive matter. Mailed on receipt of 10 cents.

1909 Locomobile Cars

The "30" LOCOMOBILE - A new five passenger model with a shaft drive system, thoroughly developed through three years of road testing. The name, Locomobile, on a shaft drive car guarantees its superiority. $3500

The "40" LOCOMOBILE - A seven passenger car, safe and comfortable - ideal for family use. The logical choice of those who want a high powered car. $4500

INFORMATION ON APPLICATION

The Locomobile Company of America. Bridgeport Conn.

BRANCHES

NEW YORK — BOSTON — CHICAGO — PHILADELPHIA

1909

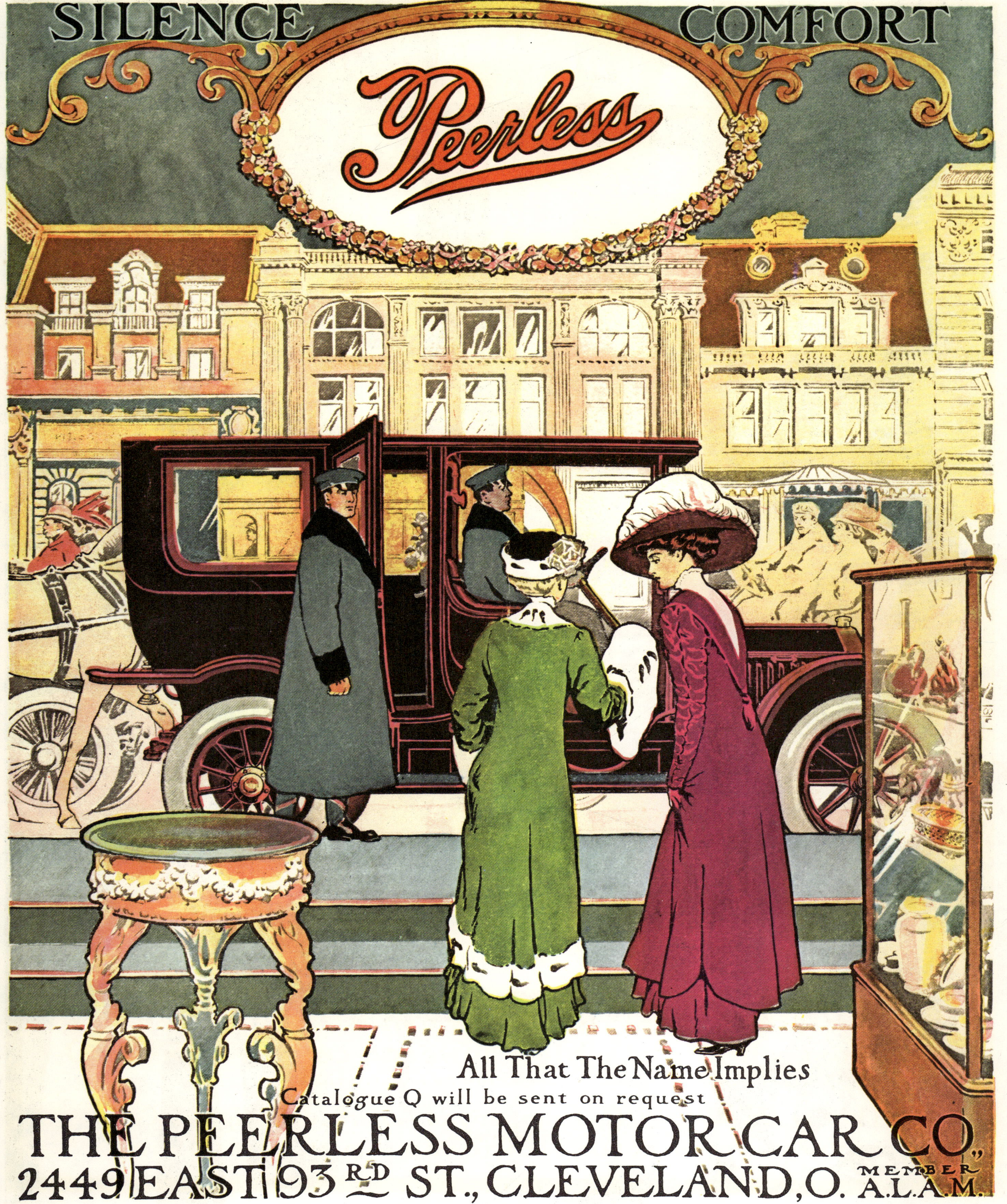
SILENCE
COMFORT
Peerless
All That The Name Implies
Catalogue Q will be sent on request
THE PEERLESS MOTOR CAR CO.
2449 EAST 93RD ST., CLEVELAND, O.
MEMBER A.L.A.M.

1909

1910

Painted by Geo. Gibbs

THE COLUMBIA MOTOR CAR COMPANY, Station 106-A, Hartford, Connecticut

LICENSED UNDER SELDEN PATENT

1910

THERE'S A TOUCH OF TOMORROW IN ALL COLE DOES TODAY

Tourster

Cole Aero-Eight

EXCLUSIVE DESIGNS - ADVANCED ENGINEERING
15000 MILES ON TIRES

COLE MOTOR CAR COMPANY, INDIANAPOLIS, U.S.A.

Creators of Advanced Motor Cars

Patent applied for

1910

1910

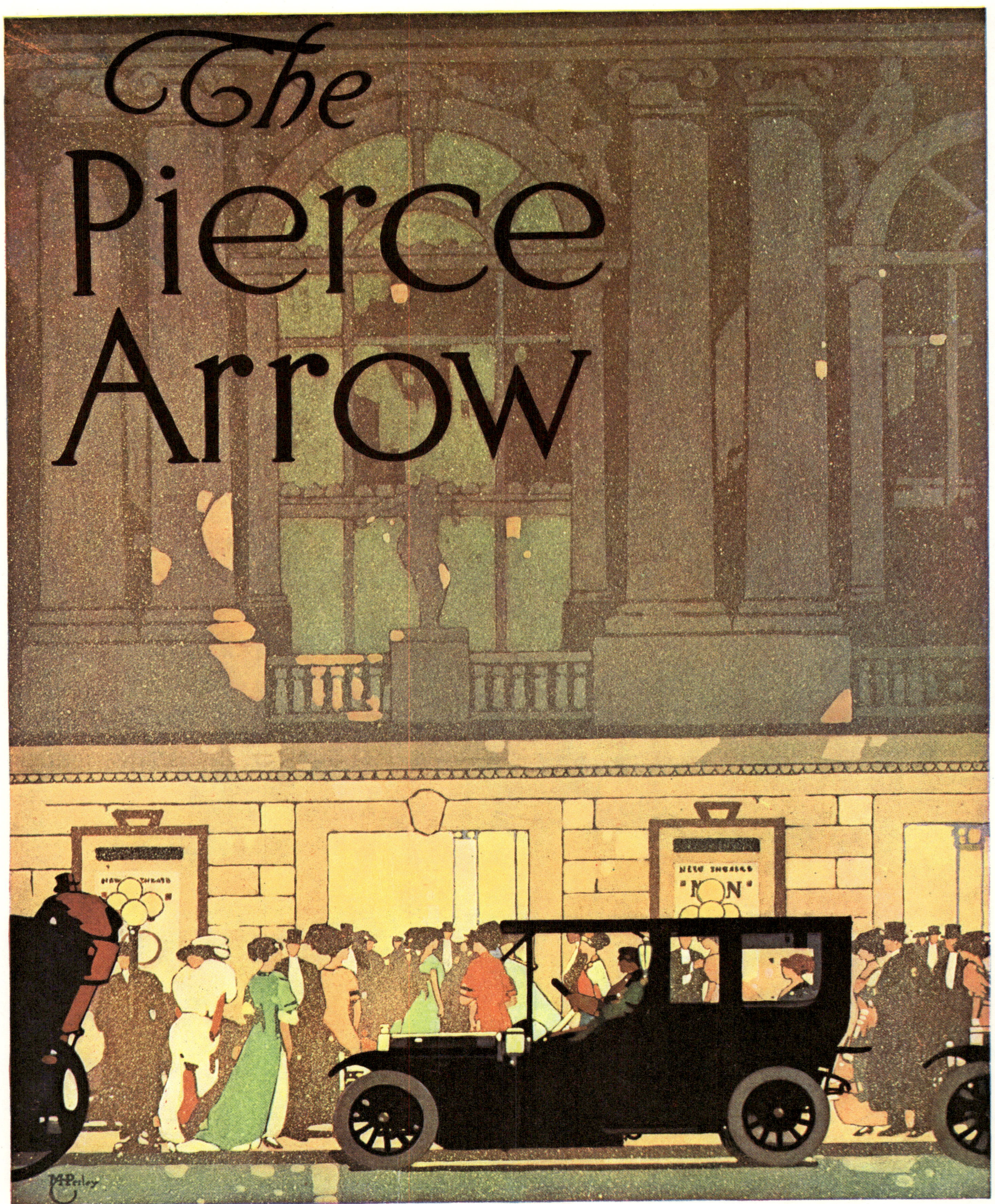

[The Pierce-Arrow at the New Theatre]

THE PIERCE-ARROW MOTOR CAR COMPANY, BUFFALO, N. Y. Licensed under Selden Patent

1911

Baker
Electrics
SHAFT
B
DRIVEN
A
Tribute
All makers of electrics would like to build a shaft driven car. It is noiseless. Maintains perfect alignment. Is graceful in appearance. People want it. But only the Baker Company has designed an efficient shaft drive for electrics. Others have experimented. The Baker has achieved. Its recent mileage record of 244½ miles on a single charge of Edison batteries is unapproached. It is the world's record.
The Baker Motor Vehicle Co.
38 W. 80th Street, Cleveland, Ohio

1911

The Pierce-Arrow at the Aviation Meet

No one thing has done so much to decrease the number of imported cars in this country as the Pierce-Arrow.

THE PIERCE-ARROW MOTOR CAR COMPANY, BUFFALO, N. Y.

Licensed under Selden Patent

1912

Catalogue N will be sent on request — All That The Name Implies

THE PEERLESS MOTOR CAR CO.,

2443 EAST 93RD ST., CLEVELAND, O.

LICENSED UNDER SELDEN PATENT

1910

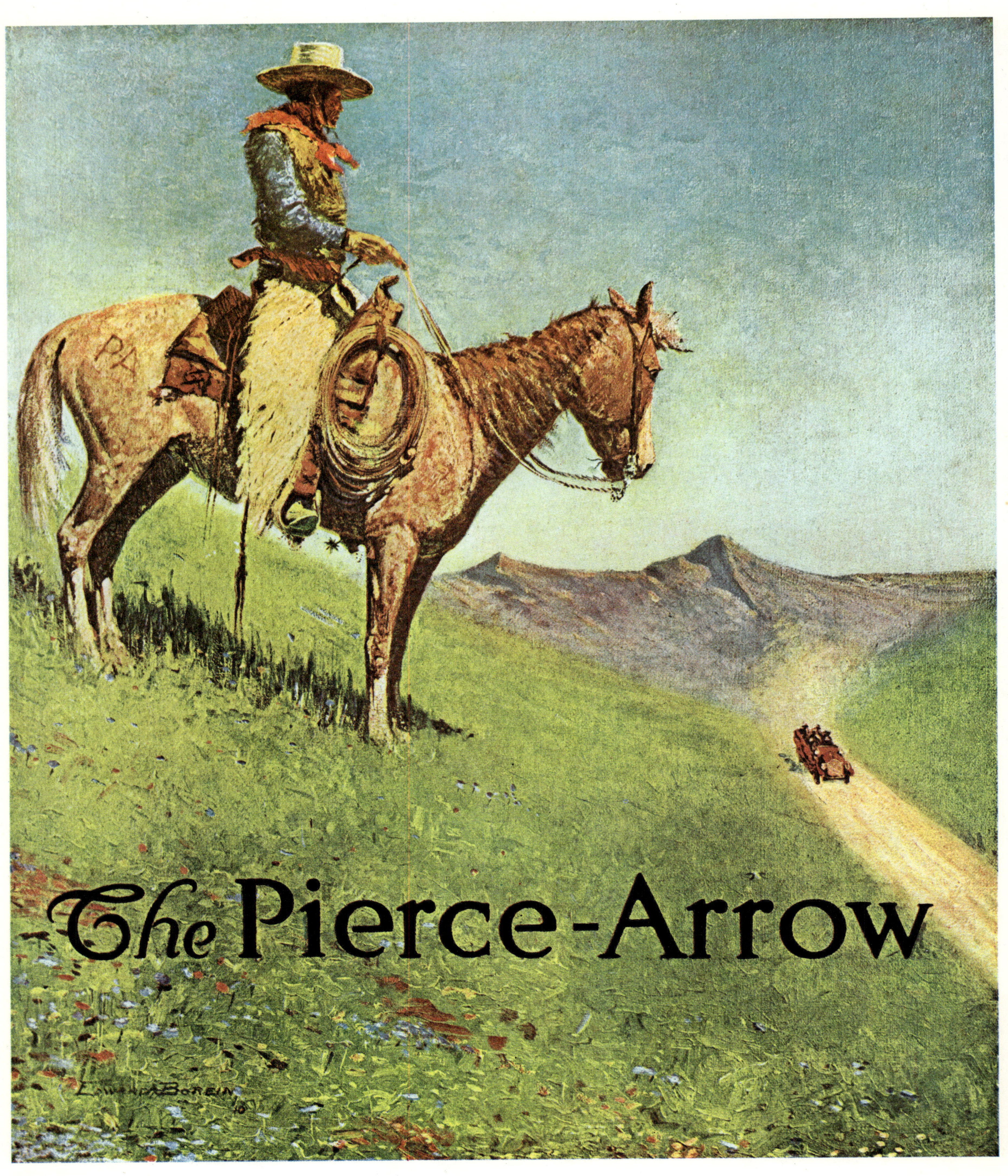

The Pierce-Arrow in the Great West

The success of the Pierce-Arrow Car is undoubtedly due to the fact that it was never built to meet a price. A successful car came first; price second.

THE PIERCE-ARROW MOTOR CAR COMPANY, BUFFALO, N. Y.

Licensed under Selden Patent

1910

A New Departure

SHAFT DRIVE

BEVEL GEAR—ON ALL

Baker Electrics

THE ONLY SHAFT DRIVEN ELECTRICS

THE GREATEST ADVANCE EVER MADE IN ELECTRIC MOTOR CARS

After many years of experimenting we have perfected a shaft drive, which excels any chain drive in efficiency, and have adopted this new transmission, because of its unquestioned superiority over every other type. This is in accordance with the practice of all high grade gasoline motor car manufacturers, both American and foreign.

WE NOW PRESENT FOR THE FIRST TIME
A COMPLETE LINE OF SHAFT DRIVEN ELECTRICS

Write for booklet giving specifications and full information regarding our many other exclusive improvements.

THE BAKER MOTOR VEHICLE CO.

38 West 80th Street CLEVELAND, OHIO

THE OLDEST AND LARGEST MANUFACTURERS
OF ELECTRIC MOTOR CARS IN THE WORLD

1909

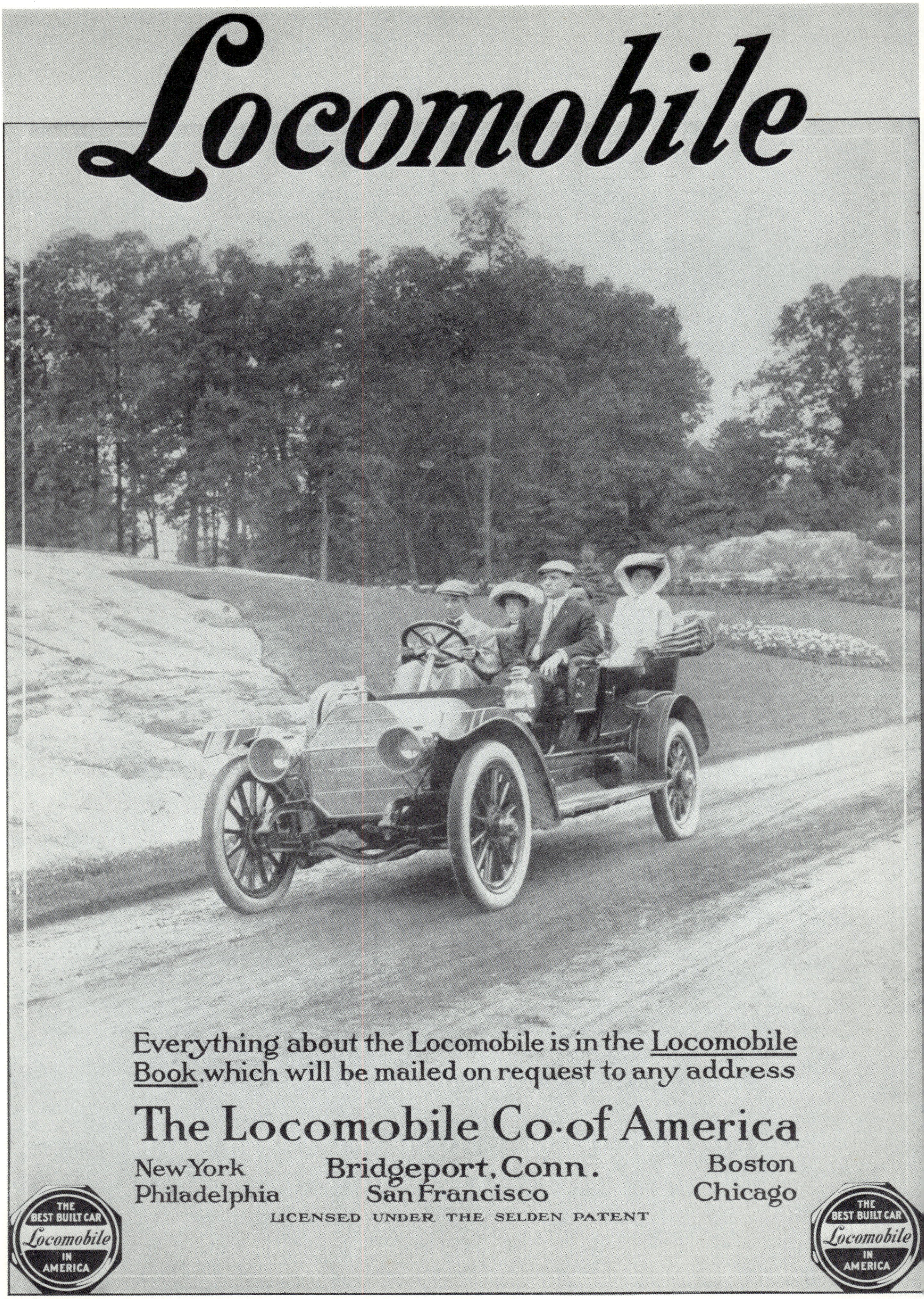

Locomobile

Everything about the Locomobile is in the Locomobile Book, which will be mailed on request to any address

The Locomobile Co·of America

New York
Philadelphia

Bridgeport, Conn.
San Francisco

Boston
Chicago

LICENSED UNDER THE SELDEN PATENT

1910

Twelve Months of Meteoric Progress

4 cylinders
20 H.P.
Sliding gears
Bosch magneto

Hupmobile

$750
(F.O.B. Detroit)
Including three oil lamps, horn and tools

Hundreds of people were undoubtedly impressed a year ago by the mere smartness of the Hupmobile—its beauty, its generous size, the obvious strength of its construction, the clean-cut appearance of the power plant, the very evident use of the best materials.

It took very little motor judgment or experience to see that $750 had never bought such value before.

But in the year that has elapsed since the Hupmobile made its bow, this first judgment has been supplemented and confirmed by a series of performances which are remarkable.

The Hupmobile in contests of speed and endurance, has repeatedly shown itself to be the peer of cars of twice its power and even four and five times its price.

Early in the year it won cups and perfect scores, for instance, in the Baltimore and Detroit reliability and endurance runs.

It carried off the palm in the Buffalo fuel economy contest.

At San Francisco it made the fastest time and a perfect score in the 200-mile annual mud plug.

In its class it won the six-hour race at Brighton Beach; and on the Los Angeles motordrome turned the mile in 58 seconds.

Crossing the desert in the Phœnix-Los Angeles race the Hupmobile took its place among the larger competing cars.

It climbed to 9,000 foot elevations in the Colorado mountains; topped the peaks of the Adirondacks; it was the first car ever to negotiate Georgia's famous Stone Mountain, under its own power, and the second to ascend Mount Greylock, Massachusetts.

In the dead of winter—through the season's deepest snows and severest cold—three Hupmobiles were driven from Detroit to New York; while in the West a tour, under conditions equally severe, was made for 800 miles from North Dakota into Canada.

The Hupmobile is today without an equal in its class, as it was the day the first Hupmobile left the factory at Detroit.

It is prized alike by the man who owns but one car—the Hupmobile—and the man whose private garage houses the costliest types of American and foreign manufacture.

It has made possible the joys of motoring to hundreds who, of necessity, awaited the coming of such a car as the Hupmobile.

Your ideals of motor car construction may be high; but you will find them realized in the Hupmobile.

If you have the engineer's love for fine machinery—the expert's admiration for skillful workmanship—you will take your hat off to the Hupmobile.

It remains the most remarkable car the industry has produced.

HUPP MOTOR CAR COMPANY, Desk 24, DETROIT, Michigan

Licensed under Selden Patent.

1910

The more different cars you own or use the more firmly are you convinced of the supremacy of FIAT. It is no exaggeration to say that the standard of motor car merit amongst buyers of judgment, the world around, is the

The FIAT car is perfected by the finest engineering skill in the world, and every FIAT—no matter what the price—is a model of FIAT excellence and FIAT value.

A FIAT car completely equipped—£500 and no extras.

In the FIAT "Light Fifteen" (developing nearly 30 actual H.P.), all-round efficiency in the hands of the amateur has been the first consideration from the drawing office to the road test and has been the object attained in this model. It is essentially the car for general use in town and country. Fitted with beautifully designed and finished landaulette body—completely equipped in every detail—it is a perfect model of FIAT value—ready for the road. It costs complete, £500 and no extras.

The standard tyre fitted to all FIAT cars is the one we consider best—MICHELIN

See the FIAT Stand, No. 38, at Olympia.

Models from 12 h.p. to 50 h.p. Prices from £325 to £1,000

FIAT MOTORS, LTD.

Telegrams: "Fiatism, London." Head Offices & Showrooms: 37-38 Long Acre, London, W.C. Telephones: 7946, 7947, 7948, 7949, 7950 Gerrard

The FIAT "Light Fifteen" Single Landaulette, as described above.

1910

Matheson

"Silent Six."

A tried and proven chassis of remarkable workmanship. Bodies by Brewster and Quinby, the latest and most luxurious examples of the art.

1912

The Social Prestige of a Baker Electric

is the result of years of refined usage by women who want and will pay for the best. Its graceful design gives the car a marked distinction. Its noiseless shaft drive and luxurious ease of riding fit it pre-eminently for social uses.

Equipped with either lead or Edison batteries (50 cells A4 or 40 cells A6), whichever purchaser may prefer.

1911 Models now being delivered. See them in salesroom of our agents in your city, or write for illustrated catalogue.

THE BAKER MOTOR VEHICLE COMPANY

39 West 80th Street :: CLEVELAND, OHIO, U. S. A.

Agencies in the Principal Cities

1910

A Town Car a Woman Can Crank

THE sole objection to gasoline cars for women's driving has been the difficulty in cranking the engine. Every White Car has a compression release which makes cranking so easy a child can do it, and without danger of back fire. This one feature alone would make the White Coupe distinctive, but it has a door on either side — the driver's seat folds up to make entrance easy from either side, and it seats comfortably three or four persons besides the driver.

The White Coupe

Everywhere the White Coupe appears — whether it be in the shopping district of our most metropolitan cities, or in the parks — it immediately arrests attention by its beauty; it is an aristocratic, elegant looking car, with a snugness all its own. Its equipment is refined — it is electrically lighted and the upholstery and little accessories are all of the finest imported materials. Money cannot buy better — in fact, a woman's wants have been studied and nothing has been omitted that could contribute to her personal comfort.

Let us send you to-day our booklet on town cars which tells a more intimate story of these cars.

868 EAST SEVENTY-NINTH STREET, CLEVELAND

THE PRESIDENT OF THE UNITED STATES
USES THE
KLAXON
ON HIS OFFICIAL WHITE STEAMER

To the motorist who has not used a KLAXON, its harsh, metallic blare often seems unnecessary. But the motorist who has used one knows that no other signalling device ever used on an automobile compares with it as an insurance against collision and an aid to sustained speed.

To the KLAXON user, blind crossings and hidden turns are virtually non-existent: his approach is heralded in ample time for unseen traffic to make way. Heavy vehicles going the same way are signalled long before they are overtaken, and turn out in season to require no slackening. On steep, winding hills a KLAXON may be the sole protection against disaster.

The value of the KLAXON as a safeguard and a time-saver for the conservative motorist was never better attested than in its adoption by President Taft on the White House automobile.

LOVELL-McCONNELL MFG. CO., Manufacturers
NEWARK, NEW JERSEY

THE KLAXON COMPANY, Sole Distributors for U. S. A.
1 MADISON AVENUE, NEW YORK.

1910

11-F
Four-Door Touring Car
with Top $3125

"Stoddard-Dayton"

In design the most impressive car in all motordom. In efficiency and dependability not surpassed by any. Six straight years of success. Every year our output has been sold out, and hundreds of orders returned we could not fill. Besides the "50" Four-Door Touring car shown above we also have the "40" of almost identical lines, but with capacity for but five passengers; with Top, for $2520; and also the "30", with Top, for $1850

The Dayton Motor Car Company
Dayton, Ohio

Our Booklet "W" shows 29 models $1175 to $4200

1910

At the seashore, in the mountains, at the country club,
on the boulevards, wherever you meet people
of wealth and discrimination–there, in
increasing numbers, you find THE
LOZIER
1912
6-CYLINDER 51HP. $5,000
4-CYLINDER 46HP. $4,700
Catalog and name of nearest dealer on request
LOZIER
2307 Mack Avenue Detroit

1911

Columbia

"One of the THREE BEST cars built."

WHEREVER fashionable people gather, there you will find the Columbia car. Its use is a mark of distinction—a proof of one's appreciation of the niceties, the refinements, the comforts of life.

The Columbia Motor Car Company
Hartford, Connecticut
Member A. L. A. M.

1911

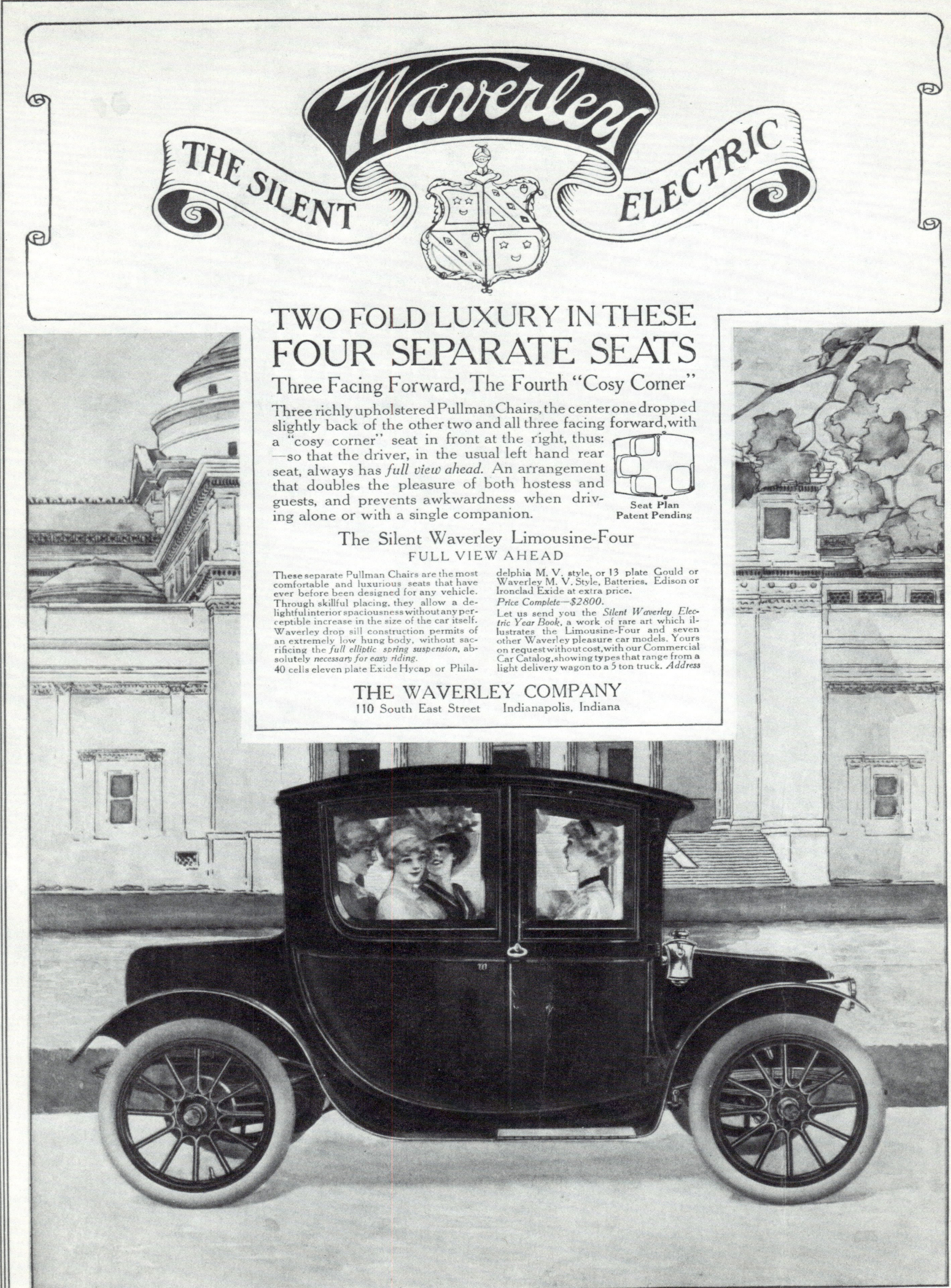
Waverley
THE SILENT ELECTRIC
TWO FOLD LUXURY IN THESE
FOUR SEPARATE SEATS
Three Facing Forward, The Fourth "Cosy Corner"
Three richly upholstered Pullman Chairs, the center one dropped slightly back of the other two and all three facing forward, with a "cosy corner" seat in front at the right, thus: —so that the driver, in the usual left hand rear seat, always has full view ahead. An arrangement that doubles the pleasure of both hostess and guests, and prevents awkwardness when driving alone or with a single companion.
Seat Plan
Patent Pending
The Silent Waverley Limousine-Four
FULL VIEW AHEAD
These separate Pullman Chairs are the most comfortable and luxurious seats that have ever before been designed for any vehicle.
Through skillful placing, they allow a delightful interior spaciousness without any perceptible increase in the size of the car itself. Waverley drop sill construction permits of an extremely low hung body, without sacrificing the full elliptic spring suspension, absolutely necessary for easy riding.
40 cells eleven plate Exide Hycap or Philadelphia M. V. style, or 13 plate Gould or Waverley M. V. Style, Batteries. Edison or Ironclad Exide at extra price.
Price Complete—$2800.
Let us send you the Silent Waverley Electric Year Book, a work of rare art which illustrates the Limousine-Four and seven other Waverley pleasure car models. Yours on request without cost, with our Commercial Car Catalog, showing types that range from a light delivery wagon to a 5 ton truck. Address
THE WAVERLEY COMPANY
110 South East Street Indianapolis, Indiana

1912

My Farewell Car

By R. E. Olds, Designer

Reo the Fifth --- the car I now bring out --- is regarded by me as pretty close to finality. Embodied here are the final results of my 25 years of experience. I do not believe that a car materially better will ever be built. In any event, this car marks my limit. So I've called it My Farewell Car.

My 24th Model

This is the twenty-fourth model which I have created in the past 25 years.

They have run from one to six cylinders—from 6 to 60 horsepower.

From the primitive cars of the early days to the most luxurious modern machines.

I have run the whole gamut of automobile experience. I have learned the right and the wrong from tens of thousands of users.

In this Farewell Car, I adopt the size which has come to be standard — the 30 to 35 horsepower, four-cylinder car.

Where It Excels

The chiefest point where this car excels is in excess of care and caution

The best I have learned in 25 years is the folly of taking chances.

In every steel part the alloy that I use is the best that has been discovered. And all my steel is analyzed to know that it meets my formula.

I test my gears with a crushing machine — not a hammer. I know to exactness what each gear will stand.

I put the magneto to a radical test. The carburetor is doubly heated, for low-grade gasoline.

I use nickel steel axles with Timken roller bearings.

So in every part. The best that any man knows for every part has been adopted here. The margin of safety is always extreme.

I regard it impossible, at any price, to build a car any better.

Center Control, Finish, Etc.

Reo the Fifth has a center, cane-handle control. It is our invention, our exclusive feature.

Gear shifting is done by a very slight motion, in one of four directions.

There are no levers, either side or center. Both of the brakes operate by foot pedals. So the driver climbs out on either side as easily as you climb from the tonneau.

The body finish consists of 17 coats. The upholstering is deep, and of hair-filled genuine leather. The lamps are enameled, as per the latest vogue. Even the engine is nickel trimmed.

I have learned by experience that people like stunning appearance.

The wheel base is long — the tonneau is roomy — the wheels are large — the car is over-tired. Every part of the car — of the chassis and the body — is better than you will think necessary. No price could buy anything better.

Price, $1,055

This car — my finest creation — has been priced for the present at $1,055.

This final and radical paring of cost is considered by most men as my greatest achievement.

It has required years of preparation. It has compelled the invention of much automatic machinery. It necessitates making every part in our factory, so no profits go to parts makers.

It requires enormous production, small overhead expense, small selling expense, small profit. It means a standardized car for years to come, with no changes in tools and machinery.

In addition to that, by making only one chassis we are cutting off nearly $200 per car.

Thus Reo the Fifth gives far more for the money than any other car in existence. It gives twice as much as some

But this price is not fixed. We shall keep it this low just as long as we can. If materials advance even slightly the price must also advance. No price can be fixed for six months ahead without leaving big margin, and we haven't done that. The cost has been pared to the limit.

Catalog Ready

Our new catalog shows the various styles of body. It tells all the materials, gives all specifications. With these facts before you, you can easily compare any other car with this Reo the Fifth.

If you want a new car you should do that. Judge the facts for yourself. Don't pay more than our price for less value. After 25 years spent in this business, here is the best car I can build. And the price is $1,055. Don't you think you should know that car?

Write now for this catalog. When we send it we will tell you where to see the car. Address —

R. M. Owen & Co. General Sales Agents for **Reo Motor Car Co., Lansing, Mich.**

Canadian Factory, St. Catharines, Ontario

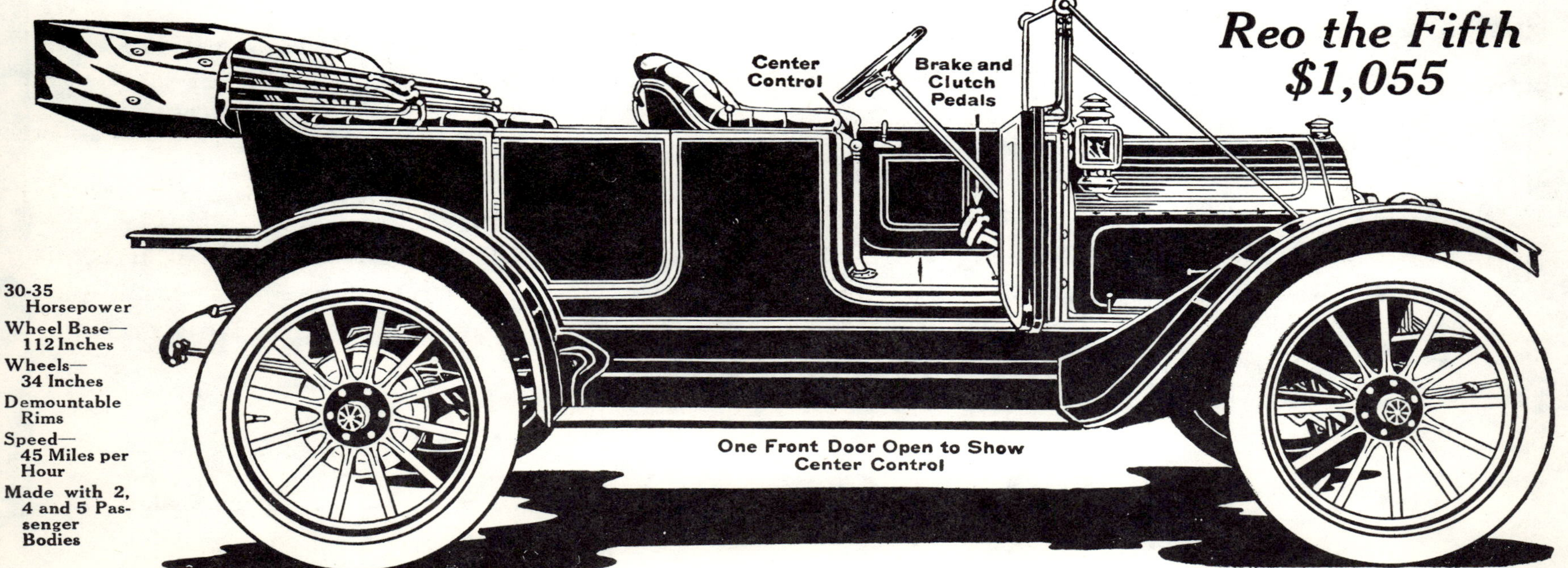

Top and windshield not included in price. We equip this car with mohair top, side curtains and slip-cover. windshield, gas tank and speedometer — all for $100 extra. Self-starter, if wanted, $25.00 extra.

THE PACKARD WAY

THE OLD WAY

Convenience, Security, Maximum Service
Packard Left Drive Motor Carriages

The New "38"   The New "48"

LEFT DRIVE

Packard left drive, with electric self starter and centralized control, means this to you:

You enter the car directly from the curb.
You avoid muddy pavements and the dangers of passing traffic.
You start the motor by touching a button and pressing a foot pedal.
You control all the lights and the carburetor adjustments from the driving position.
When driving in traffic you have an unobstructed view of the road ahead.
When turning off to the left in traffic, your protection is assured by a position convenient for signalling with the left arm.
When turning off to the right, you are naturally protected by the adjacent curb.

ELECTRIC STARTER

The electric cranking device is an integral part of the motor. Electric starters are admittedly the best and this is proved to be the best of electric starters.

CENTRALIZED CONTROL

Centralized control is a convenience available to Packard owners alone. Starting, lighting, ignition and carburetor controls are on the steering column within easy reach of the driver's hand and are operated without leaning forward or moving in any way from a driving position.

UNEXPECTED emergencies demand the bridge builder's factor of safety. Endurance far exceeding the requirement, is the uncompromising standard to which every Packard is built. The new "38" and the new "48" represent knowledge of emergency requirements, knowledge gained through fourteen years' experience in the factory and on the road.

Ask the man who owns one

PACKARD MOTOR CAR COMPANY, DETROIT

1913

THE Detroit ELECTRIC
IN THE past twelve months there have been twice as many Detroit Electrics sold as any other make of electric car. This greater volume reduces manufacturing costs and also reduces selling expenses—two vital reasons why we offer better cars at lower prices.
Purchasers for 1914 have their choice of worm or bevel gear axles, Detroit Duplex Drive, front or rear seat drive. New equipment includes electric hand brake, longer wheel base, yet a 12-foot shorter turning radius than heretofore; larger tires, increased battery capacity (washing unnecessary); all battery cells accessible by raising hoods; Hanlon patented rain-vision shield, oval crowned fenders and deep Turkish cushions.
Note the Prices:
With Bevel Gear Axle
Victoria $2800
4-pass. Brougham Rear Seat Drive 2550
5-pass. Brougham Front Seat Drive 2800
With Worm Gear Axle
Gentleman's Roadster $2500
4-pass. Brougham Rear Seat Drive 2850
5-pass. Brougham Detroit Duplex Drive 3000
(Prices f.o.b. Detroit)
These cars are on exhibition at our branch offices and selling representatives of the Company in over 175 cities. Demonstrations gladly furnished any time.
Send for our new catalog in colors.
Anderson Electric Car Company, Detroit, U. S. A.
Builders of the "Detroit Electric"
Largest manufacturers of electric pleasure vehicles in the world.
Detroit

1913

Pierce-Arrow

PIERCE-ARROW TOURING LANDAU IN THE TYROL

THERE is not made to-day anywhere in the world a car more perfectly meeting all demands than the PIERCE-ARROW car.

THE PIERCE-ARROW MOTOR CAR COMPANY, BUFFALO, N. Y.

1913

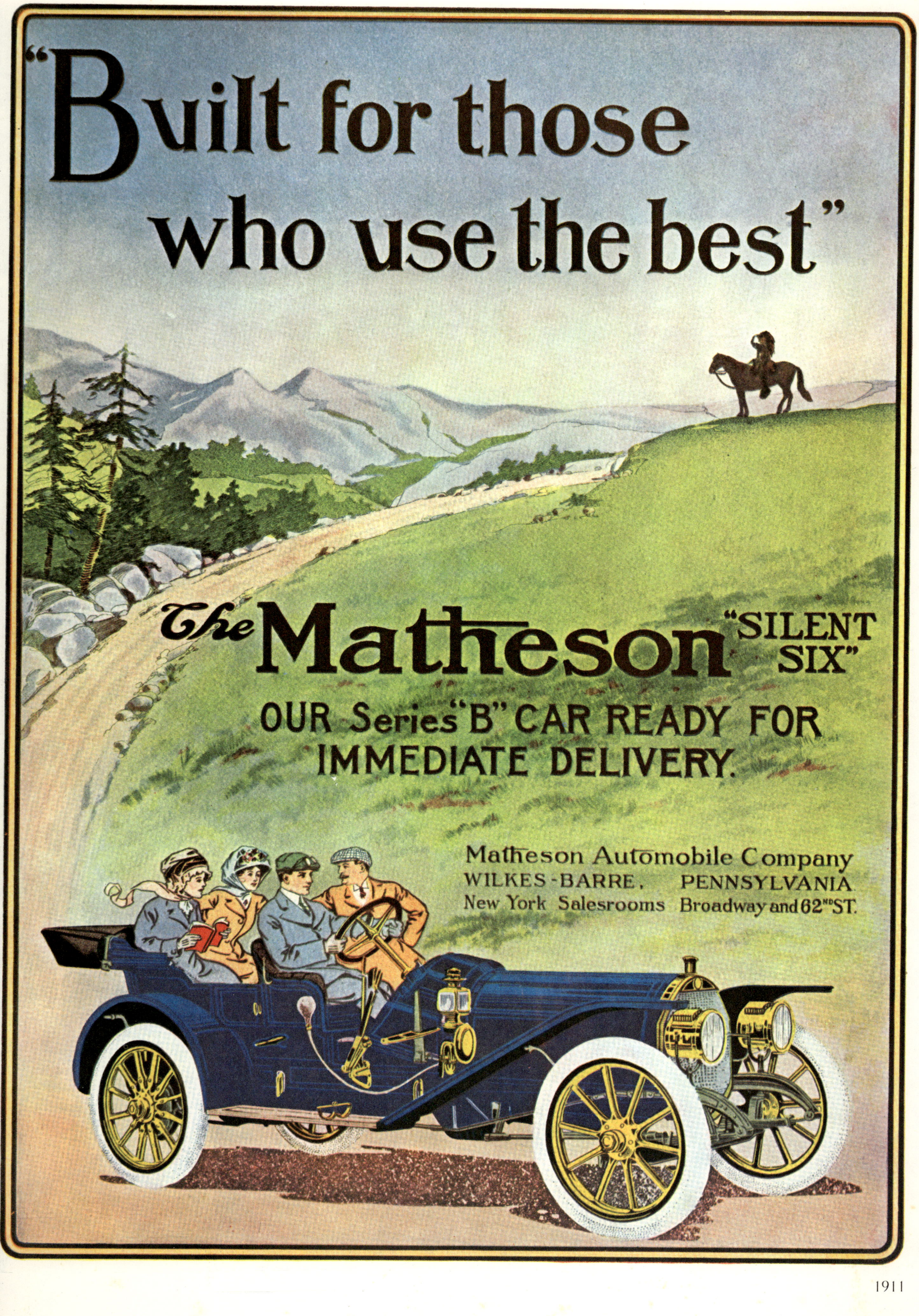

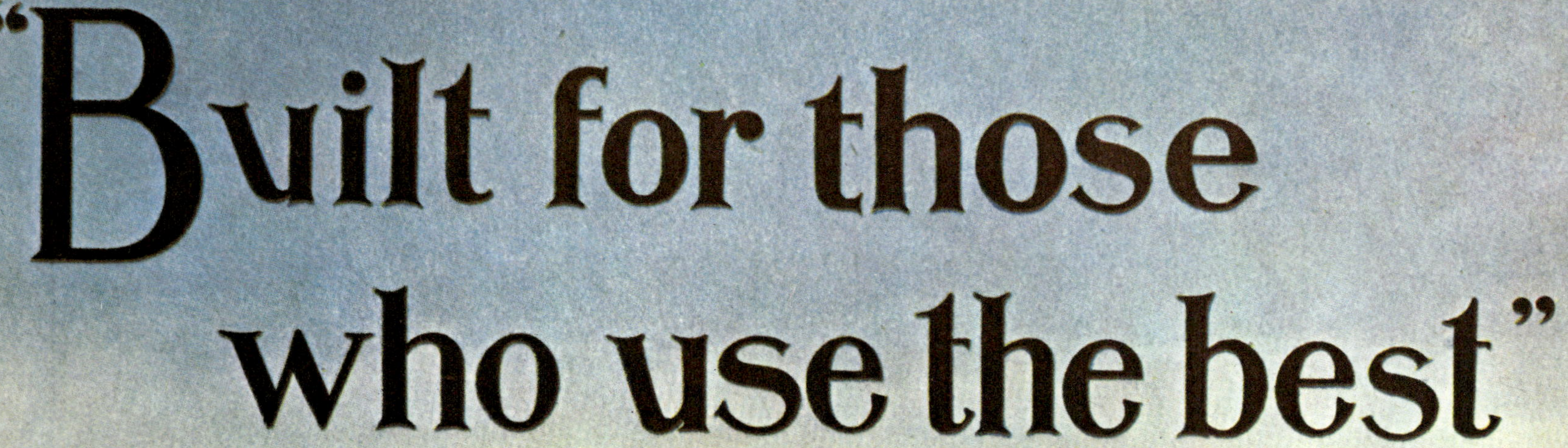

"Built for those
who use the best"
The Matheson "SILENT SIX"
OUR Series "B" CAR READY FOR IMMEDIATE DELIVERY.
Matheson Automobile Company
WILKES-BARRE, PENNSYLVANIA
New York Salesrooms Broadway and 62ND ST.

1911

The Pierce Arrow

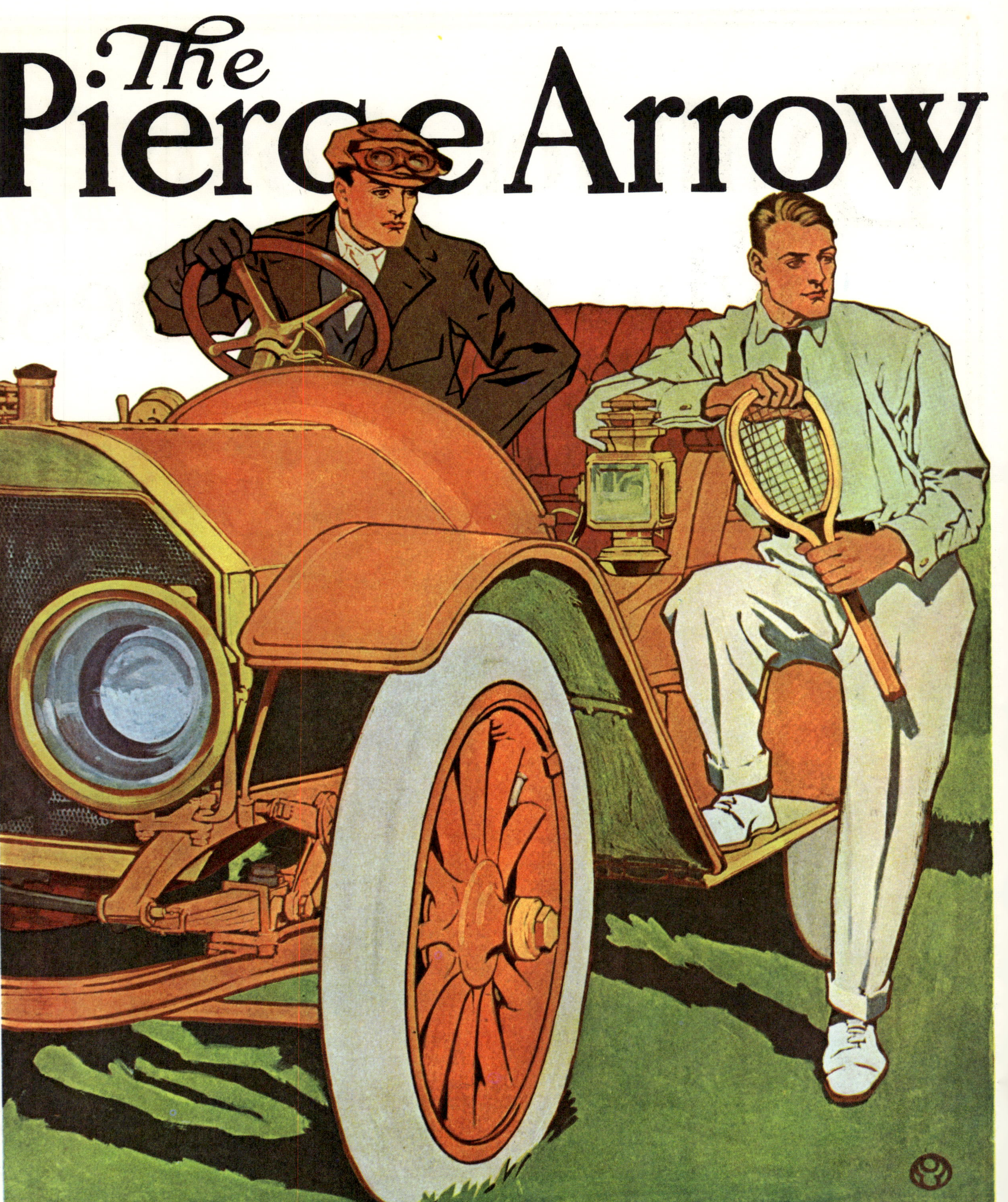

THE six-cylinder idea is no more a rightful adjunct of the Pierce-Arrow Car than are a hundred other sound ideas of car construction that we have adopted after a thorough trying out. Luxury means efficiency always.

THE PIERCE-ARROW MOTOR CAR COMPANY, BUFFALO, N. Y.
Licensed under Selden Patent

1910

The Limited started right.

Here is a brief, "inside" history of the most remarkable high-powered six-cylinder automobile ever produced.

In 1906 we made plans to build an Oldsmobile "Six" which should be actually superior to all existing types, in touring comfort, speed, silence and reliability.

In 1907, after exhaustive shop tests, the first car was completed and road tests began. In 1908 an officer of the company drove a finished car many thousand miles.

In the course of these try-outs, the running gear received as much consideration as the motor. It was found that, within certain limits, the larger the diameter of wheels and tires the more luxurious were the riding qualities.

In 1909 regular deliveries to the public were made. Then the wheel diameter was increased and the famous 42-inch tires became the standard equipment. The output was over-sold.

Veteran motorists were amazed at the riding qualities revealed by the large tires. Ruts, bumps and cobble-stones seemed to disappear by magic. Record high mileages were secured, sometimes treble the previous average.

The Limited of today, with its wonderful, long stroke motor and a multitude of improvements and refinements, is far ahead of the Limited of 1907. By the same token, it is ahead of other six-cylinder cars.

Although the seven-passenger touring car now runs on 43 x 5 inch tires, it is designed so skillfully that body, bonnet and wheels are in proper artistic proportion. The center of gravity is low, entrance and exit are made easy and all the lines are graceful and pleasing.

While daringly original five years ago, the principles of its construction were sound, so we may say that—

The Limited started right, has been perfected to the utmost—and is today without serious competition.

Touring, Tourabout, Roadster and Limousine bodies. Prices, $5000. to $6300. The Oldsmobile catalogue describes all styles of the Limited, the Autocrat and the Defender. Sent gratis.

OLDS MOTOR WORKS, LANSING, MICHIGAN

Branches in the Principal Cities. *Dealers from Coast to Coast.*

Stevens-Duryea
"Nearly a Quarter-Century of Leadership"
So profoundly beautiful are the lines of the new Model C-Six Stevens-Duryea enclosed bodies that they compel the admiration of the conservative buyer of fine cars.
In their creation a marked advance has been made upon present types and they are instantly recognized as not only elegant but distinctive.
Open and enclosed cars $4500 to $5950
Catalogue on request
Stevens-Duryea Company
Chicopee Falls Mass
"Pioneer Builders of American Sixes"
THREE POINT SUPPORT
UNIT POWER PLANT

1916

LOZIER
At the country club, on
the boulevards, at the seashore,
in the mountains, wherever you meet
people of wealth and discrimination–
there, in increasing numbers you find
the LOZIER
1912 6-CYLINDER 51 H.P. $5,000–4-CYLINDER 46 H.P. $4,700
Catalog and name of nearest dealer on request
LOZIER, Detroit
Frank X. Leyendecker

1912

Stevens-Duryea individuality appears not only in the lines of the car but in the thorough-going comfort that is possible only because of the three-point support of its power-plant.

The comfort is real, and so is the reason — told clearly in our "Individuality" book. Send for it.

Stevens-Duryea Company Chicopee Falls Mass

"Pioneer Builders of American Sixes"

THREE POINT SUPPORT — UNIT POWER PLANT

1912

"Autocrats" of the Road

There's as much solid comfort in the two-passenger Touring Roadster and four-passenger Tourabout as there is in our seven-passenger cars.

The contour of seats and cushions;
the depth and quality of upholstering;
the room allowed for legs and elbows;
the protection from dust;
the arrangements for ventilation;
the wheel-base and drop frame;
the large wheels and tires;
the springs and shock-absorbers;—

plus the long stroke, smooth running engine, — all produce Comfort, in superlative degree.

Formerly one expected luxury and room in limousine and touring cars — but a certain amount of dust and cramped quarters in a roadster. Oldsmobile designers, however, studied the possibilities of these smaller types for a long time, and each year an advance was made, culminating in the Autocrat models shown above; — literally the "last word" in cross-country luxury!

Exclusive features worth noting are; — the dust-screened wind-scoop and "sky-light" in the hooded dash; patent Oldsmobile ventilators in fore doors; enclosed, bull's-eye side lights (wired to battery), and the convenient luggage and spare tire arrangements.

Tourabout $3,500

Engine and Chassis the same as for Autocrat Touring and Limousine bodies.

Touring Roadster $3,500

Equipment absolutely complete and of the highest possible quality.

The Oldsmobile catalogue is a handsome book, showing all types and styles of Oldsmobiles. It will be sent gratis, on request.

OLDS MOTOR WORKS, LANSING, MICHIGAN

Branches in the Principal Cities. Dealers in every section from Coast to Coast

1912

LOZIER
ON touring highways, at the seashore, on the boulevard in the mountains, at the country club,—wherever you meet people of wealth and refinement, there, in increasing numbers, you find the Lozier.
Big Six. Touring Cars $5,000, Limousines and Landaulets $6,500.
"LIGHT SIX" $3,250 to $4,450.
LOZIER MOTOR COMPANY
232 Mack Avenue
Detroit, Michigan
Factory Branches in New York, Chicago, Boston
Philadelphia and San Francisco

1913

Model 42, five-passenger touring car, $1750. Top and windshield extra.

True Mechanically—Truly Artistic

¶ In 1913 Oaklands beauty is given a new charm, luxury a new significance and individuality a new meaning.

¶ All that you care for in a motor car is found in the Oakland. All of the best and certain of the old and all that is safe and beautiful in the new, has found a place in the Oakland for 1913.

¶ Fours and Sixes, in a wide range of body designs. $1000 to $3000.

The Greyhound 6-60 — wheel base 130 inches, double drop frame, unit power plant, cone clutch, sliding gear transmission, full floating rear axle, demountable rims, "V" shaped German silver radiator, 10-inch upholstering, full nickel trimmings and equipped with the improved Delco electric lighting, starting and ignition system, $2,550. (Top and windshield extra.) There is mounted on this chassis four, five and seven passenger bodies and a raceabout for two. Price of all models the same.

Model 42 Chassis — 116-inch wheel base, double drop frame, unit power plant, cone clutch, sliding gear transmission, full floating rear axle, demountable rims, "V" shaped German silver radiator, 10 inch upholstering, full nickel trimmings and equipped with the improved Delco electric starting, lighting and ignition systems, $1750. (Top and Windshield extra.) There is mounted on this chassis a five passenger body, a close coupled four passenger body and the famous Sociable Roadster (three passenger single seat). Price of all models the same. There is also built a smart four passenger coupe on this chassis selling for $2,500.

Model 35 Chassis — five passenger touring car, wheel base 112 inches, unit power plant, demountable rims, storage battery for electric lighting, nickel trimmings, $1075. We are also building on this chassis a three passenger Sociable Roadster, at $1,000. Model 35 will be equipped with electric lighting and ignition system and air starter at a nominal charge.

Write for Catalogue and booklets "What the Car With a Conscience Stands for" and "The Oakland Your Car for 1913"

OAKLAND MOTOR CAR COMPANY,
PONTIAC, 140 OAKLAND BOULEVARD MICHIGAN.

1913

1913

1913

1914

THE PIERCE-ARROW CAR

Our idea is that the car should go "there and back" in the shortest possible time, with the least trouble to both owner and driver, with the greatest comfort to the owner in transit, at the least expense, weight of car and equipment considered, and without interruption of the trip by reason of or the fault of the car, and that it should do this not only now and then, but always. That is the service that the Pierce-Arrow Car is planned to perform.

The Pierce-Arrow Motor Car Company, Buffalo, N. Y.

1914

Pleasure
—and your Rauch & Lang or Baker Electric is a car of Pleasure.
You find pleasure in the utility by which you so easily reach the out-o'-way places or make a social call.
Pleasure in the ease of control—in the roomy interior, in the genuine coach work, and in the knowledge that your car *is* a Rauch & Lang or Baker Electric.
THE BAKER R & L COMPANY
Cleveland, Ohio
Rauch & Lang Electrics
"The Social Necessity"
Baker Electrics
QUALITY SERVICE

1916

$1485 *Milburn* $1485

f. o. b. Toledo — f. o. b. Toledo

LIGHT ELECTRIC

NEVER was any other Electric such an unqualified success as the 1915 Milburn.

Never before was there such beauty, such style, such comfort, such lightness, such speed and mileage, at anywhere near the price—$1485.

This season there are many improvements.

The Milburn is now faster than ever and it now travels even more miles per charge.

And many minor refinements make it a smarter and even more efficient car.

Though Milburn lightness caused a general lightening of Electrics, the Milburn is still by far the lightest.

Though the Milburn price caused a general lowering of prices, the Milburn is still by far the lowest cost Electric — both first cost and operating cost. See the Milburn dealer at once.

Write to us for our catalogue.

THE MILBURN WAGON COMPANY

Established 1848

The Milburn Electric Charger solves the home-charging problem—effectively—inexpensively—if your public garage is inconveniently located or lacking in electric facilities.

TOLEDO, OHIO

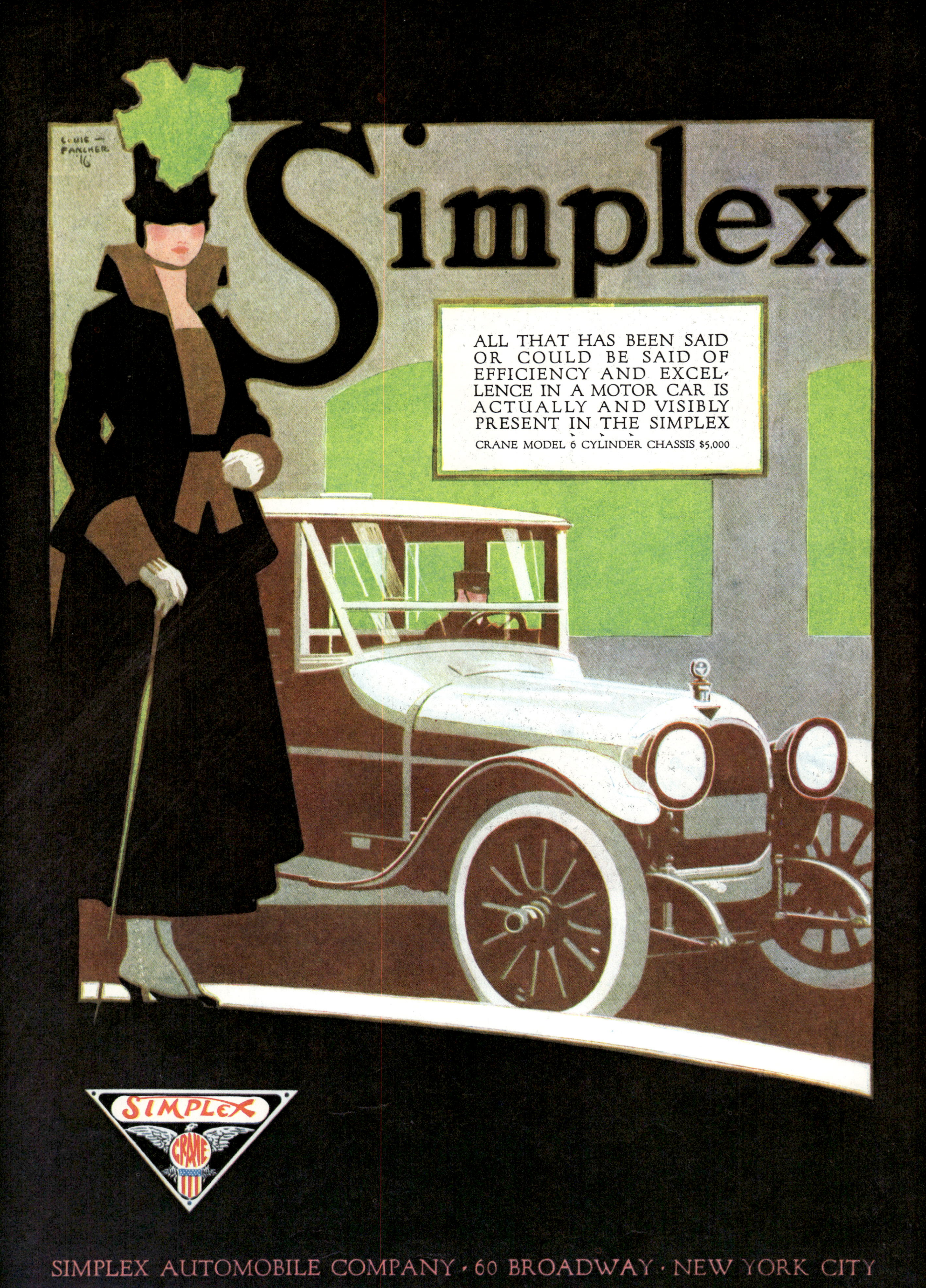
LOUIS FANCHER '16
Simplex
ALL THAT HAS BEEN SAID OR COULD BE SAID OF EFFICIENCY AND EXCELLENCE IN A MOTOR CAR IS ACTUALLY AND VISIBLY PRESENT IN THE SIMPLEX
CRANE MODEL 6 CYLINDER CHASSIS $5,000
SIMPLEX
CRANE
SIMPLEX AUTOMOBILE COMPANY · 60 BROADWAY · NEW YORK CITY

1916

$2,550, f. o. b. Detroit—Seats Six

Luxury's Limit

The Car With a Thousand Charms

Forget for the moment that the Limousine described here sells this year for $2,550. We are facing new price standards in upper-class cars. The time is past when luxury lovers need suffer over-tax.

The Famous Chassis

This is the new-model HUDSON Six-40—the latest production of Howard E. Coffin, America's foremost designer.

Mr. Coffin, with the 47 other engineers, has devoted four years to this model. It is their final conception of the ideal Six.

It excels in lightness, in economy, in beauty and equipment. In many ways it is the finest example of the new-day quality car.

And the size is just right for ease of handling, combined with ample room.

The Artistic Side

This Limousine body is built for us by famous New England coach builders. Every detail shows the artist's touch.

It is upholstered and trimmed in finest imported fabrics. Sample books at your local HUDSON showroom will offer you four options.

The hardware is hard-rubber-covered. That is, door handles, window lifts, etc. The rear doors lock.

There are all the dainty appointments—toilet cases, smoking cases, electric light in the dome, electric telephone to driver.

All the glass is sashless. Window and door lights may be dropped. The sashless glass back of the driver is adjusted for ventilating. Set it at any height.

The windows and doors have roll curtains. Roll-up storm curtains protect the front seats.

The extra seats are collapsible, and one may set them to face either front or rear.

All This for $2,550

Here is a car which is widely considered the prince of modern Sixes. In every part and detail it denotes our level best.

It comes with a Limousine body built by masters of the art. It is luxurious to the last degree.

Now, for the first time—because of HUDSON efficiency—this highest class of closed car is offered for $2,550.

Go judge for yourself—at your Hudson showroom—if any car at any price offers more that you desire.

Hudson dealers are everywhere.
New catalog on request.
7-Passenger Phaeton sells for $1,550.
3-Passenger Roadster sells for $1,550.
3-Passenger Cabriolet sells for $1,750.
4-Passenger Coupe sells for $2,150.
Canadian Prices: Phaeton and Roadster, $2,100 f. o. b. Detroit, Duty Paid.

HUDSON MOTOR CAR COMPANY, 8208 Jefferson Ave., Detroit, Mich.

(197)

BOSS OF THE ROAD

A NEW PACKARD—THE "4-48"

This latest Six is the larger consort of the Packard "2-38." The "4-48" has all the refinement and luxury of the "2-38," plus a bigger margin of reserve power. Twenty styles of bodies, open and enclosed.

THE DOMINANT SIX FOR EXTRAORDINARY SERVICE

The Packard "4-48"—Six cylinders, cast in two blocks of three. Bore, 4½ inches; stroke, 5½ inches. Wheelbase, 144 inches. Tires, 37 by 5, front and rear, non-skids on rear. Seven-bearing crank shaft. Packard worm bevel driving gears.

Standard equipment of the Packard "4-48" includes Packard one-man top, Packard windshield, Packard-Bijur electric lighting and starting system, Packard control board, speedometer and clock, power pump for inflating tires.

Catalog on Request

PACKARD MOTOR CAR COMPANY, DETROIT

LINCOLN HIGHWAY CONTRIBUTOR

The "2-38" Phaeton, $3750
The bows supporting one-man top are so arranged as to leave the view entirely unobstructed in the forward portion of the car.

The "4-48" Salon Touring Car, $4850
This style, which is distinguished by individual front seats with passageway between, carries six passengers. The Standard Touring car seats seven.

1914

Baker Electrics
QUALITY SERVICE
Rauch & Lang Electrics
"THE SOCIAL NECESSITY"
PERSONAL PRIDE
PRIDE of ownership has always marked the possession of a Baker or Rauch & Lang Electric.
¶ It denotes an appreciation of that deft touch in master design and workmanship so exclusively characteristic of every Baker or Rauch & Lang car. Quality alone can bring this comfort of mind—this pride of possession. That is why the Baker or Rauch & Lang cars justly command the price which those who know and want only the best are willing to pay.
The Baker R&L Company
Cleveland, Ohio

1915

Whito
Custom-built

The Semi-Touring Car

Easily converted from an open touring car into a fashionable turnout, completely enclosed. The tonneau then presents the refined interior of a limousine body, with perfect protection against weather In quality and design, a custom-built product.

The WHITE COMPANY
CLEVELAND, O.

Upholstery and finish may be selected to suit the owner's individual taste.

1916

Unequalled *for* Convenience—*for* Economy—*for* Service

When it blows—
When it rains—
When it's dusty—
When it's cold—

And the minute it blows, rains, gets dusty or ld—then you want protection—instantly.

That's why, for most climates—for most occa-ons—for most people, the closed car is the best r to own.

There are few occasions when any other type of r would serve you better.

There are many occasions when no other type car will serve you so well.

And among closed cars there are none so permanently reliable and economical to own and drive as these Willys-Knight models.

They cost less to buy because the economies made possible by huge production are here applied to closed car prices.

They cost less to drive because they have the sleeve-valve motor—the most economical motor the world has ever known.

Not only is the sleeve-valve motor the most economical in consumption of gasoline for the power it delivers—

But it will stand more use—even abuse—without mechanical attention or adjustment, than any other motor ever devised.

And it will outlast by many thousand miles any other type of motor.

These are not mere claims—they are universally admitted facts.

There is nothing experimental about the sleeve-valve motor—nothing new except the low price made possible by quantity production, for the first time in these cars.

Ask anyone who owns a sleeve-valve motored car if he would consider for a minute going back to any other type.

His answer will make you want to see the Overland dealer to order one of these cars now.

The Willys-Overland Company, Toledo, Ohio

"Made in U. S. A."

1916

The Car of a Hundred Quality Features that created a new standard of automobile value. The ALL-YEAR Touring-Sedan, Coupe-Roadster and Victoria-Town Car are mounted on the famous *Hundred Point Six*. Prices $1520 to $1850. Open touring and roadster bodies without the ALL-YEAR feature $1095.

Send for ALL-YEAR Car booklet just issued

Kissel Motor Car Co.
Hartford, Wisconsin, U. S. A.

The ALL-YEAR Car—Detachable Sedan Top mounted on HUNDRED POINT SIX Five Passenger Gibraltar Touring Body and same car with top detached. Price complete $1520.

1916

Overland

TRADE MARK REG.

Light Four $695

Big Four $850

f.o.b. Toledo

1917

The FRANKLIN CAR
FIND a man who has experienced the luxury of a Franklin Sedan for summer use.
Ask him what he thinks of the Enclosed Car idea for summer.
He will tell you that he has made a discovery in motoring; that he will never use any other type of car.
He will tell you that the lightness and resilience of the Franklin Sedan make it practical for any kind of driving, on any sort of road, any time, anywhere.
That he gets all the free-blowing air there is—as much or as little as he wants. That he can instantly adjust the windows for any sort of weather—shut out dust or rain; drive for fifty miles on a hot summer afternoon and step out of the car clean and cool.
Then he will tell you what it means to his wife and family. The freedom from grimy, parched skins and enveloping veils; the joy of stepping on to a hotel veranda without looking like the rescued survivors of a wrecked Cook's Tour.
Then he will come back to the flexibility of the Franklin, the lightness of its unsprung weight. Easy riding over rough roads, liveliness on the hills, maximum speed from place to place, economy in gasoline, remarkable tire-mileage.
Features that apply as well to the Brougham and Cabriolet Models as to the Sedan—the features that make the Franklin so definitely an all-around efficient car.
Franklin Sedan (5 passengers) 2610 lbs. $2850.00
Franklin Brougham (4 passengers) 2575 lbs. $2800.00
Franklin Cabriolet (3 passengers) 2485 lbs. $2750.00
All Prices F. O. B. Syracuse
FRANKLIN AUTOMOBILE COMPANY
SYRACUSE, N. Y., U. S. A.

1917

Lexington
MINUTE MAN SIX
The Perfected Six
¶ The Greater Lexington Minute Man Six—a bear for power, a lamb for docility—is a universal favorite.
¶ The only motor dead gas cannot choke, one-finger emergency brake, beautiful body lines, and 22.8% more power with greater fuel economy are some of its exclusive features made possible by basic and far-reaching improvements.
¶ Ten great, specialized factories contribute to its finished perfection, making its excess value possible at its reasonable price.
Series "R" Five Passenger Touring Car with two auxiliary seats
$1585
All prices f. o. b. factory and subject to change without notice
Lexington Motor Company, Mfrs.
Connersville, Ind., U. S. A.

1918

PAIGE
The Most Beautiful
Car in America
WE HAVE set out determinedly to produce the last word in ultra-luxurious enclosed vehicles—all our own original creations.
Three remarkable engineering features—peculiarly Paige—that eliminate "starting troubles" and insure smooth running in all temperatures, combine to make these vehicles the Most Comfortable of Winter Cars—as well as The Most Beautiful Cars in America.
PAIGE-DETROIT MOTOR CAR CO.
DETROIT

1918

An Inevitable Decision

Whatever your ideals today, you are certain to come to the conclusion sooner or later, that an enclosed automobile, like the Rauch & Lang Electric, is the ideal.

For it combines all the desirable features while eliminating the crude. Noise and vibration are absent. Likewise all the well-known annoyances and much of the expensive upkeep incident to gasoline cars.

The Rauch & Lang Electric is unlike old-time electrics. We, too, have progressed. So there is more mileage, more speed, maximum economy. There are utilitarian reasons sufficiently predominating to make every man and woman want to know and understand this superior automobile before deciding *which* enclosed car.

Each Rauch & Lang Electric represents the finest traditions of the coach builder's art. No car is handsomer. Nor more comfortable. A descriptive and illustrative catalog will be sent upon request.

The Baker R & L Company, Cleveland

Builders of Custom Coach Bodies of Quality

1919

New Series Haynes Brougham—five passengers. Cord tires and wooden wheels standard equipment on all six cylinder cars. Cord tires and five wire wheels standard equipment on all twelve cylinder cars. Disc wheels optional equipment, at an extra charge, on all models.

This advertisement copyrighted, 1920, by The Haynes Automobile Company.

The NEW *Series* HAYNES BROUGHAM

ROMANCE, social distinction, traveling luxury—these distinguished the Brougham in the old days of fine coaches and colonial manners.

In creating the new series Haynes Brougham, all the richness of appearance and supreme comfort of travel have been restored, with the added improvement of motoring flexibility and power.

The charming lines of the body appeal as much as do the wide doors, the deep-upholstered divan which forms the rear seat, the exquisite fittings and all the other thoughtfully incorporated conveniences which are so greatly admired by car connoisseurs. Exteriorly the new series Haynes Brougham conveys an expression of richness, exclusiveness and dignity. The new series Haynes Brougham seats comfortably five passengers.

The Haynes, America's first car, now exhibited by the Government at the Smithsonian Institution, National Museum, Washington, D. C., was invented, designed and built by Elwood Haynes, in 1893.

The beautiful Haynes Brochure, descriptive of all the new 1920 and new series Haynes character cars, will be mailed to you upon request. Address Dept. 466.

THE HAYNES AUTOMOBILE COMPANY
KOKOMO, INDIANA . . . . U. S. A.

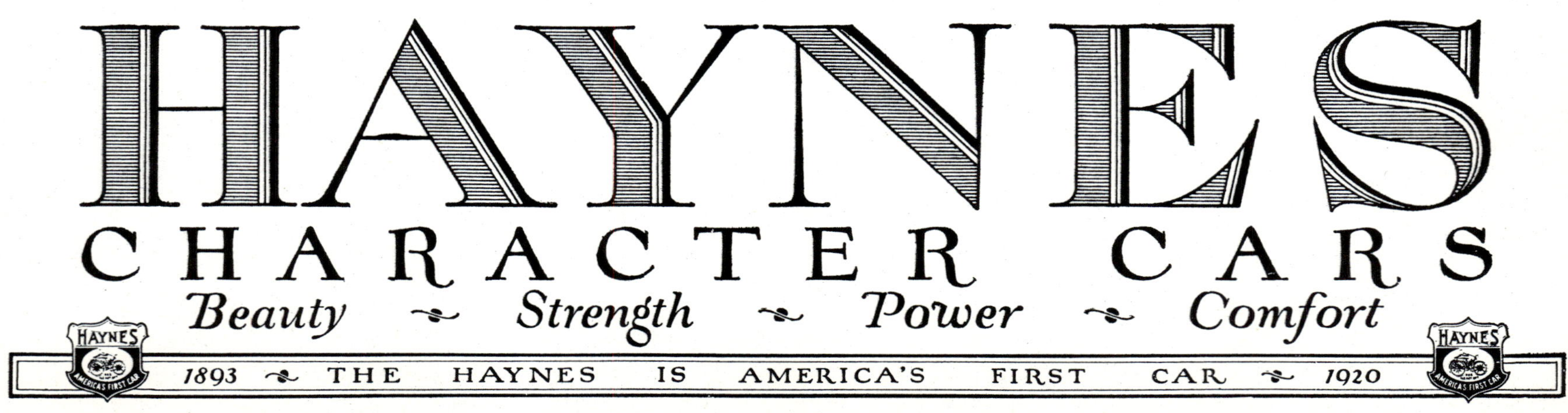

1920

INDIANAPOLIS
STUTZ
INDIANA, U.S.A.
The Car That Made Good in a Day

1920

SPEED~ENDURANCE~POWER-
EXPRESSED IN DUPONT
DESIGN AND REALIZED IN
DUPONT PERFORMANCE
DU PONT MOTORS INC., WILMINGTON, DEL.

1920

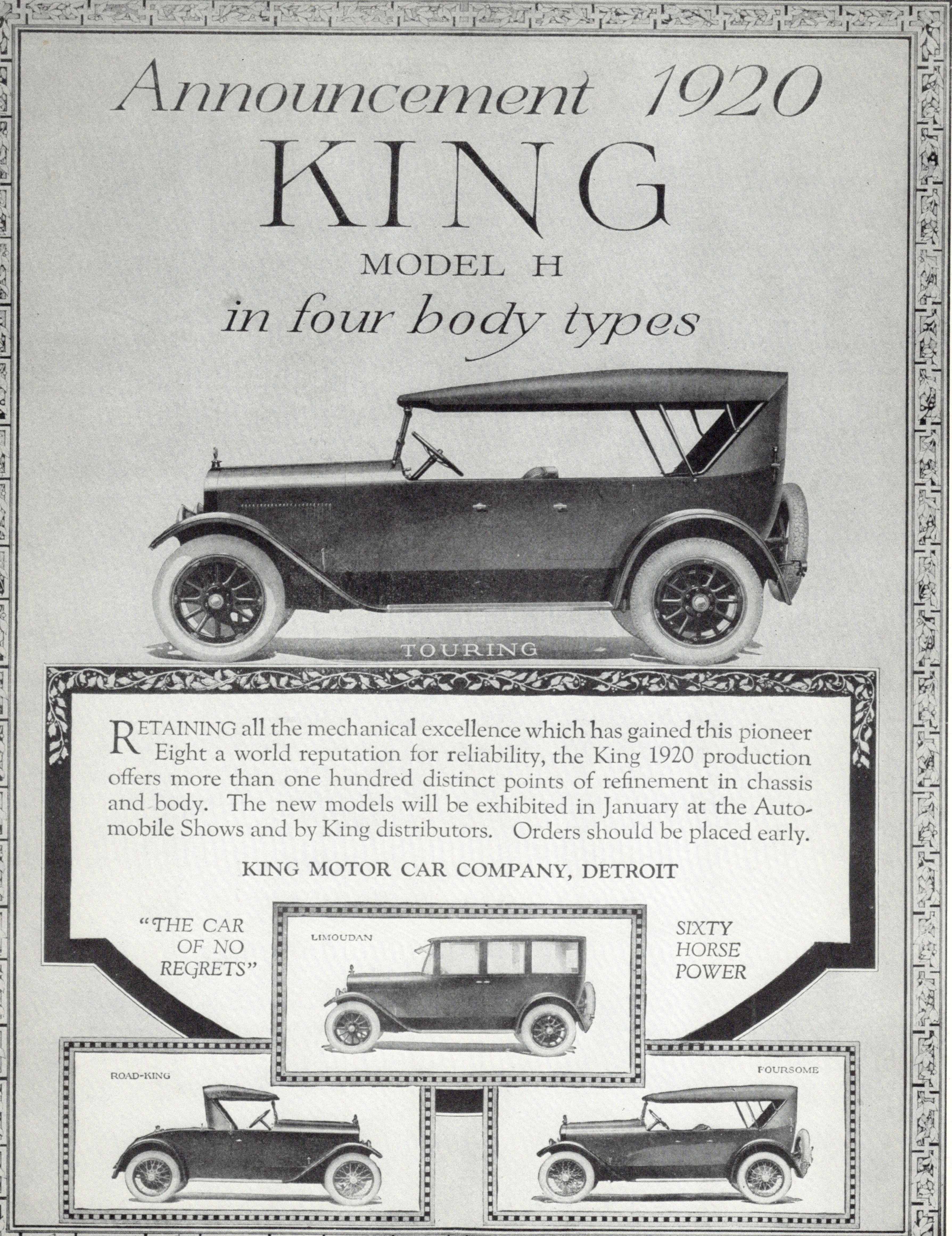
Announcement 1920
KING
MODEL H
in four body types
TOURING
RETAINING all the mechanical excellence which has gained this pioneer Eight a world reputation for reliability, the King 1920 production offers more than one hundred distinct points of refinement in chassis and body. The new models will be exhibited in January at the Automobile Shows and by King distributors. Orders should be placed early.
KING MOTOR CAR COMPANY, DETROIT
"THE CAR OF NO REGRETS"
LIMOUDAN
SIXTY HORSE POWER
ROAD-KING
FOURSOME

The ROAMER
America's Smartest Car
IN THE Roamer models for 1920 your desire for finer beauty and distinction in a motor car has found its fullest expression. Here is rare subtlety of line and color, with a fund of power equal to any test confronted.
The privilege of selecting finish, color, appointments and upholstery, granted to each purchaser; imparts further distinction and individuality.
The Roamer brochure for 1920 will be sent upon your request.
BARLEY MOTOR CAR COMPANY,
1910 Reed St. Kalamazoo, Michigan
A limited number of Deusenberg-motored Roamers are now available.

1920

GIOVANNI
BOY VIOLINIST
Arriving in Style
Baker Electrics
QUALITY SERVICE
Rauch & Lang Electrics
"The Social Necessity
Arriving at one's destination surely and safely may be accomplished with any automobile; but to arrive in style, as well as in utmost comfort, is particularly appreciated by those who know and want the best.
It is this exclusive factor of style which has particularly marked every Baker or Rauch & Lang production in every era of fashionable coach building.
Not forgetting that Baker and Rauch & Lang Electrics also embody superb engineering features that offer unusual advantages of service, safety and silence.
THE BAKER R & L COMPANY, Cleveland, Ohio

1916

Simplex
IN motors, as in clothes, the most admired and copied are those expressing the refinement and exclusiveness of the made to order. Simplex, Crane Model, 6 cylinder—Chassis $6000.
Bodies to Order
SIMPLEX AUTOMOBILE CO.
60 BROADWAY NEW YORK
SIMPLEX
CRANE

1916

The New
Willys
KNIGHT
Sleeve Valve Motor
Limousine
$1950
Model 88-4 f.o.b. Toledo
MYRON PERLEY

Smarter—Easier Riding—Quieter

Smarter then ever in its design, finish and appointments, the new Willys-Knight Limousine awaits your inspection.

Quite aside from its captivating style appeal, it has distinctive advantages which no other Limousine enjoys.

Luxurious in appearance and comfort, it is ultra-luxurious in its *quietness*.

No other Limousine is so quiet.

The mechanical noises of motors and gears have been silenced as never before.

And permanently silenced!

Important as quietness is in any car, it is doubly important in closed cars which tend to magnify all mechanical noises.

The Willys-Knight Limousine has the sleeve-valve motor—the quietest motor ever designed and the only motor which grows quieter with use.

But not only does it grow quieter—it also grows steadily more powerful and more flexible and outlasts any other type of motor ever built.

A superior motor in any car, it is beyond argument the ideal motor for closed cars—and the only motor which is free from those effects which closed bodies emphasize.

Of equal importance from the standpoint of luxurious quietness are its silent spiral bevel drive gears.

The new Willys-Knight Limousine has a longer wheelbase and cantilever rear springs which make it the easiest riding car you can imagine.

See it to-day—Overland dealers will gladly show and demonstrate it.

The Willys-Overland Company, Toledo, Ohio
"Made in U. S. A."

1916

1917

Raulang Electrics
More Men
Now Prefer the Raulang!
More and more men find the need of an enclosed car—and, in the electric, the ideal. Its wonderful flexibility enables one to wend his way quickly and safely through traffic without strain or effort. The mind is freer. One is not his car's slave.
Usual mechanical annoyances are absent. The Raulang is always ready at a moment's notice, easily operated, theft-proof, clean, roomy and comfortable.
It takes you farther than you ever have occasion to go in a day and as fast as you care to drive—faster, in fact, than the law allows. The Raulang is truly an all-family, all-hour, all-purpose automobile—the climax in simplicity and economy.
Before you buy an automobile, you owe it to yourself and your family to first investigate a Raulang. Illustrated, descriptive booklets on request.
The Baker R & L Company, Cleveland
Builders of Custom Coach Bodies of Quality

1919

MARMON
34
Founder and master of the new school of scientific car construction which has reduced the weight of the present-day automobile, increased its strength, lengthened its life and multiplied its fuel and tire mileage. Noble in grace and conduct, rapid in acceleration—long, low and powerful—1100 pounds lighter than other cars of its class.
NORDYKE & MARMON COMPANY
INDIANAPOLIS, IND.

1917

White Sixteen valve 4

A *Standard* of fine quality and design which affords infinite satisfaction. A *standard* of service which saves time and energy in these days of intensive effort. A *standard* of four cylinder efficiency which economizes fuel and operating cost.

The White Company, Cleveland

This Popular Car Exemplifies Buick Supremacy

Unquestionably this five-passenger, six-cylinder Buick touring car is the most popular and sought after high grade motor car in America.

To its rare and exceptional value is obviously due this signal success.

The fine, distinctive body lines and the perfection so evident in every detail of finish and appointment distinguish this Buick as a car of unusual grace and beauty.

The acknowledged superiority of the Buick valve-in-head motor and all the many features of Buick construction are admirably demonstrated in its ability to perform perfectly under any and all conditions.

For all the family for all purposes there is a Buick, from a light, racy roadster to a luxurious enclosed car, to fit your requirements. From $660 to $1835.

Buick D Six-45, $1070.

Buick Motor Company

Pioneer Builders of Valve-in-Head Motor Cars

Branches in all Principal Cities; Dealers Everywhere

Main Office and Factory, Flint, Michigan

(5)

QUIET when new, it grows more and more quiet with use until it reaches the point almost of absolute silence.

Smartness of appearance is accentuated by smartness of performance.

As its sleeve-valve motor "works in," carbon deposits serve only to increase its smoothness, power and efficiency.

And this many phased improvement with use will continue miles after any other type of motor would have outrun its pleasurable usefulness.

You will be well repaid if you give the Overland dealer an opportunity to show and demonstrate the Willys-Knight Cars.

In addition to the Coupe, there is the Roadster at $1095, the Touring Car at $1125 and the Limousine at $1750—all prices f. o. b. Toledo.

The Willys-Overland Company, Toledo, Ohio.

1917

Greater Beauty—Greater Dependability

Nothing like an electric!
Nothing can take its place!
Its convenience, its smartness, its cleanliness, its fitness for either winter or summer use, make it the indispensable car.
And it's no trouble to decide which electric to buy.
Of course you want a modern light, low car.

The Milburn was the first light electric —it's the time tried light electric with no hint of experiment.
It's the only light electric which is modern and stylish in appearance.
Artistically and mechanically it surpasses easily all the old fashioned high electrics which have been experimentally lightened and lowered in price to meet Milburn competition.

And it is still the lowest priced electric —a roomier, lighter, more beautiful car without hint or suggestion of experiment — time-tried and proven —for $1685.
Milburn dealers in principal cities.
If you do not know the nearest one write us and we will send you the catalogue and tell you where to see and try the car.

Established 1848 **THE MILBURN WAGON COMPANY** **Toledo, Ohio**

AUTOMOBILE DIVISION

The Milburn Town Car—outside driven—inside capacity four passengers—a beauty—$1995 f.o.b. Toledo

Write for catalogue

The Milburn Charger solves the home charging problem—inexpensively—efficiently

1917

MARMON
34

Below is pictured an exact likeness of the Marmon Limousines sold to the French High Commission for the use of the General Staff. No greater distinction has been conferred on any American car

NORDYKE & MARMON COMPANY

Established 1851

Indianapolis, U. S. A.

RF

CHALMERS

WITH HOT SPOT AND RAM'S-HORN

The temptation to over-elaboration has been avoided studiously in the interior and exterior decorative treatment of the Chalmers Limousine Landaulet, resulting in an automobile of dignified beauty, reflecting in every possible way the atmosphere of the homes of people of good taste.

CHALMERS MOTOR CAR COMPANY, DETROIT, MICHIGAN
CHALMERS MOTOR COMPANY OF CANADA, LTD., WINDSOR, ONTARIO

1919

310
THE CABRIOLET
White
Sixteen valve 4
A perfect example of custom built quality and an impressive illustration of the distinction to be attained by hand wrought, built in, refinement in every detail of body and chassis.
Upholstery and finish may be selected to suit the owner's individual taste.
The WHITE COMPANY, Cleveland

1917

DELAGE
LA VOITURE CHIC
Le Chassis $12.000
AUTOMOBILES DELAGE
DELAGE CONCESSIONNAIRES (U.S.A.) INC.
26 WEST 58th STREET, NEW YORK
Raimon. 1920

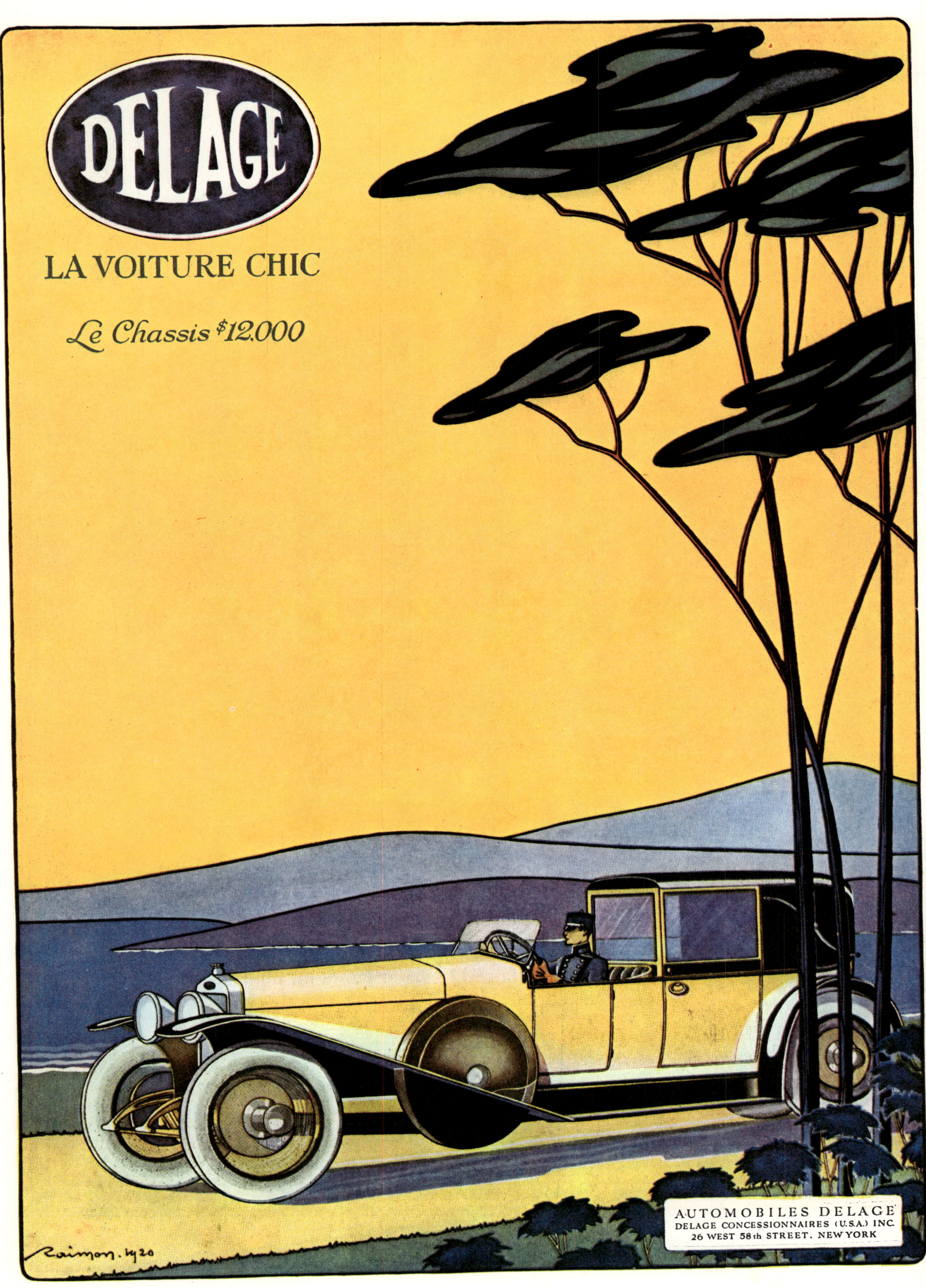

1920

RVBAY
CARROSSERIE
AVTOMOBILE
On a Marmon Chassis.
RUBAY CARROSSERIES are widely imitated but their grace of line, beauty of finish and quality of coach work are never equalled. They are designed and built by craftsmen whose artistry and workmanship are unmatched in the whole field of automobile body building.
Rubay Company
Cleveland

MARMON 34

A motor car built to a new degree of accuracy — so smooth in operation, so immune to trouble and wear as to be an entirely new experience for the motoring world. A motor car that truly reflects the great lessons we learned in building aircraft engines for the government — *that* is the new series Marmon 34.

NORDYKE & MARMON COMPANY
Established 1851. :: INDIANAPOLIS

1920